Open Source Architecture

Carlo Ratti is an architect and engineer by training.
He practices in Italy and teaches at the Massachusetts
Institute of Technology, where he directs the
Senseable City Lab. His work has been exhibited at
the Venice Biennale and MoMA in New York. Two
of his projects were hailed by *Time Magazine* as
'Best Invention of the Year'. He has been included in
Blueprint Magazine's '25 People who will Change the
World of Design' and *Wired*'s 'Smart List 2012: 50
people who will change the world'.

Matthew Claudel is a researcher at MIT's Senseable
City Lab. He studied architecture at Yale University,
where he was awarded the 2013 Sudler Prize, Yale's
highest award for the arts. He has taught at MIT,
is on the curatorial board of the Media Architecture
Biennale, is an active protagonist of Hans Ulrich
Obrist's 89plus, and has presented widely as a critic,
speaker, and artist in-residence.

Open Source Architecture

Carlo Ratti
with Matthew Claudel

 Thames & Hudson

First published in 2015 in hardcover in the United
States of America by Thames & Hudson Inc.,
500 Fifth Avenue, New York, New York 10110

thamesandhudsonusa.com

Library of Congress Catalog Card Number
2014952397

ISBN 978-0-500-34306-7

Printed and bound in China by Toppan Leefung
Printing Limited

Adjunct Editors

The authorship of this book was a collective endeavor.
The text was developed by a team of contributing editors
from the worlds of art, architecture, literature, and theory.

Assaf Biderman
Michele Bonino
Ricky Burdett
Pierre-Alain Croset
Keller Easterling
Giuliano da Empoli
Joseph Grima
N. John Habraken
Alex Haw
Hans Ulrich Obrist
Alastair Parvin
Ethel Baraona Pohl
Tamar Shafrir

Contents

Authors' Note

The ongoing project that has become this book began with a solicitation from *Domus* magazine: an editorial, by Carlo Ratti, to be published in *Domus* 948 (June 2011), a special issue on "Open-Source Design." When he was asked to write on the theme, Ratti responded with an unusual suggestion: in keeping with the open-source directive, authorship could become plural. Within a few hours, a page was started on Wikipedia, and an invitation was sent to an initial network of collaborators.

The kernel of an idea, so-called "open-source architecture," was in the hands of the group, and both the concept and its assortment of contributors expanded continually. In its online form, the text provoked widely varying responses and became the subject and object of an evolving dialogue. The article that was printed in *Domus* is a capture of the text as it stood on 11 May 2011, but the Wikipedia page remains online as an open canvas – a 21st-century manifesto, transformed by permanent evolution.

The idea continued to grow, pointing toward its full treatment in a book. Faithful to the original methodology of open sourcing, this book, *Open Source Architecture*, began in much the same way as the *Domus* article. An initial framework was the product of energetic discussion and, after words were put to page, the body of text was expanded, honed, and augmented by a group of adjunct editors from the worlds of art, architecture, literature, and theory (more information about this process and retrospective description of its *dénouement* appears in Chapter 7).

The text that ultimately emerged from all of this has an uncommon rhetorical structure. Not unlike tacking in a ship (cutting back and forth to move upwind), the argument pushes forward vigorously and along different vectors. The voice carries far in one direction before swinging back in another, yet it always maintains a clear bearing and a forward thrust. That orienting vector – a common belief in the idea of open sourcing – is shared by the collective author, but an aggregate structure of chapters as self-contained arguments promotes internal *Verfremdung* (distancing) and criticism, allowing for the productive superposition of ideas among the authors and adjunct editors. *Open Source Architecture* invites a constant reassessment of the rhetorical direction, as its voice moves from monochord to choral. Beyond the internal alchemy, we hope that this structure will solicit a critical response from the reader as well.

1

....

The Promethean Architect:
A Modern(ist) Hero

The first right on earth
is the right of the ego.

Ayn Rand, "*The Soul of an Individualist*," 1961 [1]

Le Corbusier's hand hovers, as relaxed and self-assured as that of Michelangelo's God creating Adam; it is the hand of the artist, touching the spark of life into a new world.

Le Corbusier (Charles-Édouard Jeanneret-Gris, 1887–1965) unveiled his vision on a crisp fall day in 1925, at the Exposition Internationale des Arts Décoratifs et Industriels Modernes in Paris. Two enormous models, each one hundred square meters, showed the Swiss architect's 1922 *Ville contemporaine*, a modern city for three million inhabitants, and his subsequent *Plan voisin* (1925), a business district in the heart of Paris. These works were not part of a larger exhibition or even an installation filling an entire room – they could only be presented in their own free-standing structure, which he titled *Le Pavillon de l'esprit nouveau* (Pavilion of the New Spirit).

It was autonomous, free, unencumbered by cultural reference or even traditional means of display: as Le Corbusier himself had stated, "modern life demands – is waiting for – a new kind of plan."[2] This was not "architecture," by any traditional definition, nor was it design or building or abstruse theory. Here, after his incendiary manifesto of 1923 – *Architecture or Revolution!* – Le Corbusier's word became flesh.[3]

The concept of the *Ville contemporaine* was simple: erase Paris's dense and convoluted encrustations of built space, leaving only Notre Dame cathedral as a memory of the past. Advances in technology would be mobilized to usher in an age of systematic, efficient buildings, and to improve the standard of living. This city of the future would be realized as multi-use cruciform towers, laid out in an orthogonal grid on the *tabula rasa* of a formerly cluttered, unproductive, and socially rotting city.

The *Pavillon de l'esprit nouveau*, as a whole, was a comprehensively designed architectural manifestation of Le Corbusier's new social theory. "On the walls were methodically worked out plans for cruciform skyscrapers, housing colonies with staggered lay-outs, and a whole range of types new to architecture that were the fruit of a mind preoccupied with the problems of the future."[4] All of this – a sweeping vision of entirely new modes of habitation – from the fecund mind of a single architect.

Le Corbusier's authorial voice echoed from architecture to furniture to theory, across the very functioning of society itself. He dreamed of implementing mass production in new ways, creating pure forms for every dimension of a standardized – an idealized – life. He understood that "the sphere of architecture embraces every detail of household furnishing, the street as well as the house, and a wider world still beyond both."[5] When it came to creating a context for human lives, Le Corbusier couldn't be bounded, couldn't rest on the seventh day. He sought to create "another city for another life,"[6] as Constant Nieuwenhuys proposed decades later, and spread that idea enthusiastically, whether by building or writing. The brilliance of his *Ville contemporaine* was in how each element fit precisely together in a seamless, coherent, and efficient whole: one that could be expanded and replicated ad infinitum. The Swiss had created clockwork – an elegant social machine with cogs and springs of architecture. As Tom Wolfe wrote, "Le Corbusier. Mr Purism...built a Radiant City inside his skull."[7]

• • • • • • • •

What Le Corbusier executed with grace and élan – architectural omnipotence, whether real or rhetorical – was the distilled goal of high modernism. Proponents of the movement dreamed of and fought for the expansion of the role of architecture; through the decades immediately before and following World War II, architects were empowered to influence every aspect of the human condition. Fueled by the political economy of the 20th century, the rise of the welfare state was an engine for top-down civic development.[8] Propelled by this momentum, the architect became concerned with more than simply constructing iconic buildings; rather, his purview (and architects of this era were almost exclusively male) stretched to encompass the whole of human life, even its banalities and underlying functions. He reimagined society itself.

During the first half of the 20th century, at the time Le Corbusier was working, there was a general sentiment that European culture had been destroyed by wars or had become so cluttered with nostalgic detritus as to be uninhabitable. It was on this soil that the Promethean architect alighted. He delivered the triumph of top-down, comprehensive design: everything worked. Not only did it work, but it ticked along effortlessly with the smooth grace of pure rationality – this was the authority that Le Corbusier fully assumed the day he unveiled his Pavilion, his hovering hand announcing a pure, single-minded vision…and society could not help but follow.

Yet Le Corbusier's ascension to the modernist throne was borne upon an epoch's momentum. The idea of social orchestration through a comprehensively designed environment stretches as far back as the French architect Claude-Nicolas Ledoux (1736–1806), who, tellingly, titled his own monograph *L'Architecture considérée sous le rapport de l'art, des mœurs et de la legislation* (Architecture Considered in Relation to Art, Morals and Legislation, 1804).[9] With the mandate of the king, Ledoux flexed his authorial muscles, expanding the boundaries of the architectural profession.

His masterwork was the Salines de Chaux at Arc-et-Senans (begun 1775), a royal saltworks that became the archetype of utopian masterplanned cities during the industrial era. In both organization and decoration, the complex expressed a dominion of man's rationality over the rude forces of nature: it was a crystallization of contemporary French philosophy, drawing on ideas about the natural structure of the universe and society. Architecture was at once physics and metaphysics. The plan of the saltworks is a semicircle, representing geometric purity as well as providing optimal visual access to the overseer, whose house sits at the center. Ledoux understood the facility as two interdependent systems and two geometries: the administrative directorship, including the overseer and the tax agents, which lay on the diameter of the hemisphere, and the workers' housing, which was arrayed on the perimeter. Line and arc.

Each building within this masterplanned campus clearly expressed its function in its appearance – an architectural concept, attributed to Ledoux, known as *architecture parlante* (speaking architecture).[10] The director's house looks authoritarian, the workers' houses look like workers' houses. The home of the overseer at the river source appears to be an enormous water valve – an architectural gasket through which the river rushes. Oikema, the "house of pleasure," is the unbuilt (unfortunately for the amusement of future architecture students) phallus of the saltworks.

For Ledoux, architecture was simultaneously an industrial, social and esthetic tool. It was a fully fledged attack on what he called "haphazard construction," using the artillery of rationality.[11] The project functionally produced salt, and conceptually organized man in the fractal-like mechanistic clockwork of the universe. This was Descartes' French industrial society, after all.

Yet the act of creating entire cities – and particularly the archetype of a designed social utopia – extended beyond the philosophical and political climate of 18th-century France.

Decades later, Charles Fourier (1772–1837) conceptualized the *phalanstère* (phalanstery, 1822),[12] a reproducible building type that generated a microcosmic social order within a single structure. It would be a self-contained community of approximately fifteen hundred people working together for the common good. The project was as much about social theory as architecture, the nuances of which Fourier published in his journal *Le Phalanstère*,[13] after which the structure was simply a physical manifestation of social organization. There was an emerging idea that architecture could influence every aspect of man's condition, from individual daily functions to the collective mechanism of society.

Contemporary English social theorist Jeremy Bentham (1748–1832) was inspired by his brother's similar designs for a textile mill in Russia, writing enthusiastically, "Morals reformed – health preserved – industry invigorated – instruction diffused – public burdens lightened – economy seated, as it were, upon a rock – the gordian knot of the poor-law not cut, but untied – all by a simple idea in Architecture!"[14] Bentham sought to realize this bold vision by creating a new functional order within the walls of a prison: the Panopticon.[15] The full title of *The Panopticon Writings* (published in 1791) announces that the novel typology contains the "idea of a new principle of construction, applicable to any sort of establishment, in which persons of any description are to be kept under inspection…with a plan of management adapted to the principle."[16] Just as the Salines de Chaux married geometry and social structure, Bentham's "new principle of construction" was to array prison cells (or hospital rooms, or students' desks) around the perimeter of a perfect circle and position an Inspection House at its center, both in plan and section. The overseer would be able to watch inmates at all times without their knowledge (and as a result, would not necessarily need to watch them at all times), and prisoners would work menial jobs, to the point that the prison could even turn a profit. Just like Fourier's idealized *phalanstère*, the Panopticon was a self-contained ecosphere – a totalitarian one, perhaps – but a socially-derived architecture nonetheless.

The mentality of a city as designed social framework was inherited by subsequent radical movements of the early 1900s, working not only in social, political, and economic dimensions, but also in the infinitesimal details of culture and esthetics. This was the apotheosis of *Gesamtkunstwerk* – a German term, popularized in the middle of the previous century by composer Richard Wagner (1813–83),[17] that describes a comprehensive, total work of art. The lone visionary modernist now found himself designing not only an office building, for example, but also the employees' desks, their modes of transportation, their homes, tables, chairs, and even the soup spoons they used for dinner. As the Dutch saying goes, "*Van stoel tot stad*" (from stool to city). The emerging mentality held that anything and everything could be designed...certainly a compelling mandate for the architect.

"The ultimate goal of all art is building! [...] Let us strive for, conceive and create the new building of the future that will unite every discipline, architecture and sculpture and painting, and which will one day rise heavenward from the million hands of craftsmen as a clear symbol of a new belief to come."[18] With this passionate manifesto of 1919, the messianic voice of Walter Gropius (1883–1969) turned *Gesamtkunstwerk* into a religion. This was the Bauhaus.

The Bauhaus, the "house of construction," distilled a new conception of design, an experiment in pedagogy and a proving ground for what architecture could be. Within the walls of what Tom Wolfe later described as an "exclusive compound,"[19] speculations on the future were created. Clear visions of its character sprang from the minds of students and faculty alike (ideas with as much variation as the strictures of the school's totalizing esthetic could encompass: white, rational, clean). Students participated in all subjects and collaborated vibrantly, working toward a cohesive, designed environment. Members of the Bauhaus sought to forge a new meaning for the architect of the future. All arts would come together as a single, elegant *Gesamtkunstwerk*, articulated through a top-down model of design. Students at the Bauhaus created capital-a Architecture, and it sparked a generation of visionaries compelled by the elegance and the new possibilities of a comprehensive environment.

While the academic, research-based environment of German modernism was more collaborative than its French counterpart, out of the Bauhaus and in its wake, Titans of design thundered across the architectural landscape of the 20th century – they who singularly committed great acts of pure creation. These men helped to crystalize the great Promethean myth of the architect, one that has persisted from Romantic times (Palladio, for example) through Ayn Rand's *The Fountainhead*[20] and up to today.

At once iconic and timeless, *The Fountainhead* (1943) is a novel surrounding the life of a heroic architect, Howard Roark, who makes the ultimate artistic sacrifice – choosing death, rather than betray his esthetic vision. It presents an image of the lone creator (a persona distilled from the mythologies of those 20th-century architects such as Walter Gropius, Mies van der Rohe, Marcel Breuer, Le Corbusier, and inspired by Frank Lloyd Wright, 1867–1959): brilliant, aloof, a combination of unshakeable self-confidence and the inexhaustible optimism of a being – something more than a man – empowered to save society.

The novel pinpoints the tension exemplified in the Bauhaus' hermetic enclosure or Le Corbusier's cold genius: how can the architect be part of the world around him yet simultaneously achieve unfettered innovation? The artist must unmoor himself if he is to substantiate what Le Corbusier called "a new spirit…a state of mind which has its own special character."[21] Howard Roark, the uncompromising protagonist, is crafted as a manifestation of this unadulterated creative force and is ultimately unraveled by its pivotal contradiction. The will to pure art is existentially incompatible with society.

"That man, the unsubmissive and first, stands in the opening chapter of every legend mankind has recorded about its beginning. Prometheus was chained to a rock and torn by vultures – because he had stolen the fire of the gods…. Whatever the legend, somewhere deep in the shadows of its memory mankind knew that its glory began with one and that that one paid for his courage."[22] Ayn Rand's cynosure of courage is condemned to suffer. This is understood to be the burden of the architect: enlighten humanity with the fire of the gods; rejection is only a confirmation of genius.

Far from a lone fictional account, the polarizing debate and shifting balance of power between client and architect recurs throughout the 20th century. The tide that had been gathering for decades (driven, in no small part, by the *sprezzatura* of Le Corbusier's nonchalant hand) finally reached its height. It took *The Fountainhead*'s bestseller appeal to spell it out, but suddenly it was obvious. The novel famously championed the creative genius, celebrating the architect's vigorous inspiration and autonomy in the face of philistine clients. *The Fountainhead* promoted the idea that architects should (even have a responsibility to) educate the bourgeoisie. Rand's none-too-fictional protagonist firmly cemented the stubborn resolve of architects across the globe: "If Howard Roark could put his foot down and refuse the bad taste of boorish clients, so can I," architects thought. Gradually, inch-by-inch, the enlightened designer had been gathering the authority to reform humanity through his craft, and Ayn Rand, the novelist, simply put it into words.

With a radical manifesto, and architecture presented as rhetoric, photograph, and dynamic film, Le Corbusier set in motion a shift toward the mediatization of the architect. He wrote as prolifically as he built, using both to effect a new social program. This was not necessarily unprecedented – writing and architecture have gone hand in hand since 15 BC, when Vitruvius wrote *De Architectura* (Ten Books on Architecture), through classical treatises, and continued into the 20th century. As writer Gideon Fink Shapiro has described, "The European avant-gardes of the 1920s, eager to revolutionize making and thinking for the modern world, yet lacking the means to test their ideas in practice, presented their work in numerous small but influential international journals."[23]

Indeed, Keller Easterling notes, "Modernism is a vampire. Modernism never kills modernism. It only keeps it alive. Modern is successive. Modern is finally possible often because of a new technological development or an ultimate solution. The zero-hour Promethean figure continues to challenge us to a duel. We end up writing manifestos in his image."[24]

Over the course of the 20th century, what began as modernists' manifestos became Robert Venturi's architecture for the average Joe, Deconstructivists' arcane linguistics, the eagerly-pursued "Bilbao Effect," and today's online blogs. Architecture has captured the public imagination. In 2009, Bjarke Ingels even released an "archicomic" titled *Yes Is More* – an uncannily appealing architectural graphic novel in which Ingels himself appears to explain his ideas and his work. To maintain a prolific output of written and analytical work, Ingels' alma mater, OMA (the office of journalist-turned-architect Rem Koolhaas), established a mirror operation called AMO, dedicated entirely to print products. As a self-reflexive exclamation point, or ;-) the firm presented *The OMA Book Machine* at London's Architectural Association: thirty-five years' worth of publications collated into a single, massive volume over forty thousand pages long.

Indeed, architecture today measures up to the extents of society: the architect is author of every scale and scope, from the stool to the city. He has designed the future, he has designed the present, and has even claimed the power of designing retrospectively (with Rem Koolhaas' *Delirious New York: A Retroactive Manifesto for Manhattan*, 1997). Design critic and historian Deyan Sudjic described the colossal gravity of modern architecture as both a physical and cultural phenomenon: it is a means of expressing absolute power. "In its scale and its complications, architecture is by far the biggest and most overwhelming of all cultural forms. It literally determines the way that we see the world, and how we interact with each other. For the patron, it is a chance to exert a sense of control over events. And for a certain kind of architect it offers the possibility of control over people."[25]

Architecture has swelled beyond all limits. The profession has reached a fever-pitch, culminating in the emergence of today's global architect. "This new professional wanted to be free from [the] everyday environment and its traditions, constraints, and limitations. From now on, [his] focus was on innovations and a new way of building," commented Dutch architect and theorist N. John Habraken.[26] After Ledoux, after Le Corbusier, after Howard Roark, after the ascension of the architect to near-mythic status, there is no reason for a creator to be fettered. Why should he be?

The phenomenon of "starchitecture" rides the crest of this wave. An elite cadre of the mega-famous has emerged to design the latest high-profile buildings, from international airports to contemporary art museums. In her essay "Towards a Global Architect," Beatriz Colomina wrote: "It is not just that space has collapsed with the introduction of rapid air travel; time has expanded. Le Corbusier had already foreseen the implications of this new condition for the architect. Practice is no longer local and time is continuous – almost a banality today when architectural offices with outposts in several cities around the world, connected through the Internet and by video conferencing, work 24 hours a day."[27] The architect has swelled beyond spatio-temporal human constraints.

This new, ubiquitous designer is a fulfillment of what the young provincial artist named Charles-Édouard Jeanneret-Gris invented and called *Le Corbusier.* The dreams of an entire era – global networks, architecture-as-media, speed, standardization, and efficiency – have at last come true.

• • • • • • • •

But what has architecture given us? Where is the pure clockwork of social utopias that Ledoux, Bentham, Fourier, Le Corbusier, and Gropius promised?

Architects have become isolated. In an accelerating bid to design society as well as every one of its cultural products – and finally to enlighten the public as to what it all means – the lone genius has distanced himself from that public itself.

Increasingly, the *modus operandi* is to design buildings with as much visibility and cultural importance as possible, rather than to address the questions at the root of human habitation (to say nothing of social utopias). The engine of architecture has become geared toward the privileged few: today, buildings designed by architects account for no more than two percent of global construction. Easterling has observed that "the building as a singularly authored object is responsible for a relative trickle of the world's spaces while a fire hose blasts out the rest."[28] Globetrotting starchitects have gathered what appears to be absolute control, unconditional omniscience, and supreme authority, yet their oeuvre amounts to almost nothing. They have willingly relegated themselves to a claustrophobically thin crust of global production. Power is used and abused – from master-planned cities to corporations to single patrons – yet the common denominator is a grand, iconic building or masterplan that has little to do with the vast majority of its inhabitants. It could be argued that through books, film, the Internet, and finally sheer willpower, the cultural idea and self-conception of the architect has enjoyed wild success, while architecture itself has failed both as a business model and as a tool for beneficial social change.[29] "The unspoken issue," notes Alex Haw, "is difficulty of metrics; how do you measure success if not by column inches? What social condition can be adequately geometricized?"[30]

Architectural historian Wouter Vanstiphout has contended, sharply and uncompromisingly, that "to restore architecture and planning to a position where it can have a real positive impact on society may even demand destroying the mythology of the architect as visionary."[31] In the architect's great ascendancy to mythic status, he has painted himself as a "visionary," yet in so doing he has disconnected himself from human life and extinguished the possibility of affecting it.

"Architecture has drifted into the stratosphere, where it's not even as simple as designs being produced which have no relationship to actual buildings, but it's even that the buildings that are being produced have no relationship to actual needs,"[32] Vanstiphout continued, succinctly. It is the comic irrelevance of SkyMall – the ubiquitous distributor of $29.95 numskullery – but on the very non-comic scale of billions of dollars.

Where is the upper limit? How far will architecture drift into the stratosphere before tumbling back down to reality? When will the (pure, white, rational) ideological edifice that Le Corbusier so solidly constructed finally crack?

2
········

Bottom-Up Architectures:
The Timeless Way of Building

Vous savez, c'est la vie qui a
raison, l'architecte qui a tort.
*You know, it is always life
that is right and the architect
who is wrong.*

Le Corbusier, quoted by Philippe Boudon,
Pessac: Le Corbusier, 1969[1]

The cities of Italy are diverse – from the unique canal culture of Venice to the densely twisting streets of Rome, to the hill towns of Tuscany – yet they share a common quality: intricate detail and infinite variety. Each city is an aggregation of layers, of stories, of voices, of family lines and struggles for power. It is an archaeology of experience, cemented in art, buildings, and piazzas. These cities are brought to life by the same streets that have been walked for hundreds of years; Giorgio Vasari's 16th-century Florence was younger, but no less rich in variety. Legend has it that the young Vasari (1511–74) left his small hometown of Arezzo, Tuscany, in 1527 with an artistic recommendation from the local cardinal. Upon his arrival in the thriving city of Florence, he was surrounded by a constellation of art and architecture unlike anything he had ever seen – works that defined the city's unique character. Aghast, he asked why these voices echoing through the streets – the voices of hundreds of artists and craftsmen – did not have names. Where were their signatures? Who created the Duomo?

Although he was a painter and an architect himself (his best-known work, perhaps, is the *Last Judgment* in the cupola of the Duomo in Florence, which he began in 1572 and which was completed by Federico Zuccaro in 1579), Vasari's true vision was to establish a canon of art history, linking personalities and their cultural context to specific feats of artistic creation. "There were built, then...many edifices of importance both in Italy and abroad, whereof I have not been able to find the architects,"[2] he wrote. Vasari lived at a time when the world of art was devoid of identity, and he observed a "rudeness and little desire for glory,"[3] in the men who had built and painted before him. His life's work was to dust off the foggy anonymity that surrounded artists up to his day.

Vasari's research led him to peer back one, even two generations, searching assiduously for the names and stories of his predecessors that had never been recorded. Everything he discovered was through reputation and word of mouth, and when he could only find a name, he took it upon himself to conjure (often humorous) biographies. Vasari spent the rest of his life compiling what became the first art encyclopedia – a great biographic anthology of Renaissance artists, providing a trajectory from Giotto, through Brunelleschi, and up to contemporaries Michelangelo, Da Vinci and Raphael.

This, he called *Le Vite de' più eccellenti pittori, scultori, e architettori*, known in English as *The Lives of the Artists*. In the introduction, he wrote, "the works which constitute the life and fame of artists decay one after the other by the ravages of time. Thus the artists themselves are unknown, as there was no one to write about them and could not be, so that this source of knowledge was not granted to posterity."[4] He succeeded in immortalizing those working before and around him, igniting a cultural obsession with the authorial artist – one that remains to this day. This has escalated to such a point that, today, the obsession with "originality" (and the fear of being accused of imitative work or thinking) is hard-wired into architects from the beginning of their education.[5] In short, Vasari was the champion of "the author" and *The Lives* was the genesis of a sea-change in artistic production; his missive to posterity.

• • • • • • • •

The history of human habitation is an untold epic of anonymous architecture: the nameless vernacular is a cultural expression of man's need not only for shelter, but also for status, identity, and delight. In 1965 Bernard Rudofsky (1905–88) completed an epochal study of what he called "non-pedigreed architecture," presented as a book and exhibition for MoMA in New York titled "Architecture Without Architects."[6] Rudofsky's project was at once an investigation, documentation, and celebration of vernacular architecture. The idea was uncommonly polemical for its era and location – during the heyday of modernism in New York, Rudofsky leveled a direct challenge toward the omnipotent authorial architect of his time.

Rudofsky's work hinged upon a central thesis: building a compelling case for authorless architecture as a viable means of design that has existed for thousands of years in cultures across the globe. His work introduced a new strand of architectural theory; through photographs and drawings, *Architecture Without Architects* showed that primordial vernacular building could rival the work of modern individual designers in both esthetic beauty and locally optimized functionality.[7] Just as Vasari had done, Rudofsky was pioneering a new field of academic study and giving a voice to the voiceless.

In the introduction to his exhibition, Rudofsky wrote, "*Architecture Without Architects* attempts to break down our narrow concepts of the art of building by introducing the unfamiliar world of non-pedigreed architecture. It is so little-known that we don't even have a name for it. For want of a generic label, we shall call it vernacular, anonymous, spontaneous, indigenous, rural, as the case may be."[8] N. John Habraken describes the same phenomenon with the term "natural relation," defined as, "the age-old settlement process where inhabitation and built form are one."[9] This could not be farther from the entrenched persona of the heroic modernist architect. Just as the discipline was ossifying into the rarefied formal precision of high modernism, Rudofsky trumpeted such architecture as the underground cities of Tungkwan, China, and the cliff dwellings of the Dogon tribe in West Africa.

He did not intend to provide an encyclopedic review of non-pedigreed building, but rather to dismantle the boundaries imposed by commercial, authorial architecture, and prove the validity of informal design. "It is frankly polemic, comparing as it does, if only by implication, the serenity of the architecture in so-called underdeveloped countries with the architectural blight in industrial countries.... There is much to learn from architecture before it became an expert's art."[10] He concludes that the slow trial-and-error process of adaptation offers a rich potential to achieve locally and culturally optimized architecture, and that this process pre-dates humanity itself. "It seems that long before the first enterprising man bent some twigs into a leaky roof, many animals were already accomplished builders. It is unlikely that beavers got the idea of building dams by watching human dam-builders at work...."[11]

At the root of Rudofsky's catalog of anonymous architecture lies a fundamental investigation of the origins of architecture itself. The author states it bluntly: "Since the question of the beginnings of architecture is not only legitimate but bears heavily on the theme of the exhibition," he wrote, "it is only proper to allude, even if cursorily, to possible sources."[12] Every ur-example he gives is a form of collective architecture – the act of building as a natural expression of culture – each a characteristic adaptation to a specific climate, environment, or topography. This is distinct from the idea of the "architect," and suggests a re-telling of the history of architecture that acknowledges "architecture" as a relatively minor and recent cultural invention. It is an intellectual position that Bruce Mau would later echo: "the history of the world of design is not the history of the design of the world."[13] Alastair Parvin, founder of the open-building platform Wikihouse, proposes that the evolution of building was shaped not by architects, but by the same forces of economics, politics, and technology that shaped everything else and existed long before the idea of the "architect" was conceived.[14] Habraken goes as far as to characterize the built environment itself as organic. "The term is justified because by a slow but continuous process of renewal, improvement, and adaptation of individual houses, cities had a self-generating ability. Houses functioned like living cells of a fabric."[15]

The conclusion is that architecture is intrinsically social: fixed structures (and eventually, towns and cities) coalesced as humanity moved on from the individualistic morass of nomadic hunter-gatherer culture, notes Alex Haw.[16] When prehistoric humans collected resources independently it was most beneficial to remain as distant as possible, but when someone has a nut you're willing to trade berries for, things start to change. Rudofsky imagined what could be gained by considering that genesis–condition, and charting the trajectory that proceeded from it. City-forming, he found, happened with the advent of agriculture and the beginnings of economy – labor became specialized, and objects acquired value beyond sustenance. From that point of origin, there is a clear developmental history of cities for thousands of years: it is a story of collective action, where sociability contributes more to the momentum of culture than individual action could.

Rudofsky was not alone in articulating the communal, cultural, and transformative genesis of collective architecture – other voices soon joined his, prominent among them that of historian and sociologist Lewis Mumford (1895–1990). "The chief function of the city is to convert power into form, energy into culture, dead matter into the living symbols of art, biological reproduction into social creativity."[17] In his expansive study of the evolution of architectural and urban space, *The City in History* (1961), Mumford considered architecture for its social value, rather than as a creative form or as a technological novelty. At a time when the cultural zeitgeist was eulogizing its triumphant leaps in scientific advancement, Mumford "argued that language and communication were the essential elements of civilization and that the city, where all kinds of relationships could be established, was in fact the great invention of society."[18] Urban space, then, is a story of humanity and how built form responds to it. Physical buildings represent abstract social functions: for example, palaces are intrinsically tied to rule, temples to religion, and market halls to commerce. Each sits at the center of an intricate web of culture, tradition, and human interaction specific to its own time.

The reciprocity between culture and built environment is best described by the Latin words *civitas* and *urbs*, representing an ancient distinction between, on one hand, the religious, political, and social aspects of a city, and on the other, its specific physical character. Italian scholar Marco Romano has defined them as "moral citizenship" and "material citizenship," asserting that *civitas* and *urbs* are inseparably linked, like the palm to the back of the hand.[19]

Yet the fingerprint of *civitas* is not only in landmark buildings and monuments. The city's beauty – and the majority of its area – is in its anonymous structures. The metropolis is a sum of important and anonymous buildings, each contributing to the urban feel and texture – although, in a great inequity, the artistry of the vernacular city goes unrecognized. (*Civitas* and *urbs* actually identify the very same condition that appalled Vasari, centuries ago. He believed it should be the *artifex* – artist – who creates *urbs*, not the collective tide of *civitas*.) In contrast to Vasari's author-model, the unique character of a city is the result of a vibrant social architecture, "a communal art, not

produced by a few intellectuals or specialists but by the spontaneous and continuing activity of a whole people with a common
heritage, acting under a community of experience,"[20] as architect Pietro Belluschi (1899–1994) described it. The motive force
is tradition, the aggregated weight of previous generations' architectural output.

This social, relational architecture is a continuum of
small acts of design, a "slow but continuous process of renewal,
improvement, and adaptation of individual houses...a self-
generating ability. Houses function like living cells of the fabric.
House types were never architectural inventions but came to full
bloom by interaction."[21]

The role of the architect, then, is not to conceive of and
build form, but rather to observe the built environment and seek
to understand his role in its inexorable advancement. Habraken
describes a process of architectural diagnosis: "we should
recognize that the built environment is an autonomous entity
that has its own ways, and the architect should study that and
explain how and why he can participate in a largely autonomous
process."[22]

The pinnacle of this "communal art" was achieved when
a drip of catalyst – in the form of technical innovations with
stone and graphic representation – fell into Europe's thick cultural glue, yielding the great cathedral projects of the Middle
Ages. In his extensive writings on cathedrals and their collective
design process, William Morris (1834–96) speculated that any
given project must have had some central impetus (an architect?
a benefactor?) but one who is not "puffed up with individual
pride" nor assured of his individual abilities. When the medieval
architect approached building design, it was "the thoughts and
hopes of men passed away from the world which, alive within
his brain, made his plan take form; and all the details of that
plan are guided, will he or will he not, by what we call tradition,

which is the hoarded skill of man handed down from generation to generation."[23]

There is a predetermined set of strictures and traditions defining the "cathedral" typology (cruciform plan, nave, aisles) with certain variables defined by the architect (number of spires, configuration of chapels) but the design (and construction) of any given component is the responsibility of a craftsman-builder.

On an individual level, the artisan acquired a deep knowledge of craft, such as the limits of stone, or the process of constructing a vault, from masons before or around him. This ad-hoc model was the basis of architectural historian John James' critical argument that Notre-Dame de Chartres, as a whole, conveys a sense of unity, but "when you examine the cathedral closely, you discover that the design is not a well controlled and harmonious entity but a mess...uniformity is the exception rather than the rule, inside as well as out."[24] The cathedral was likely constructed in many phases, over a span of decades, during which design decisions would have been made on the job. The result can be read as either dynamic or frenetic.

Even if such a reading of the Gothic collaborative construction process has been challenged by other research, Chartres cathedral was undoubtedly built through a multi-tier operational model (one that N. John Habraken or even Wikipedia would go on to follow centuries later): an open framework that leaves specific content-generation up to its users. The power of the crowd achieved results. Builders were not highly trained specialists, but common members of the community – they were the ones who would soon come every Sunday to worship in the very same cathedral. "They could not have had our genius-complex," wrote John James, "for they worked at what had to be done each day, without conceit."[25] It was that attitude – community, collaboration, and lack of conceit – that suggested an ethical merit within Gothic architecture.

Hundreds of years later, when English society was gripped by the Industrial Revolution and a galvanic attitude of efficient production at the expense of individuals, architect and theorist John Ruskin (1819–1900) emerged as a great champion of Gothic architecture, touting its moral superiority. He advanced his social–ethical–esthetic convictions in a multi-part essay, *The Seven Lamps of Architecture* (1849), pointing back in time to the medieval era as the paragon of beauty and truth in architecture. Two of the main tenets of architectural value (what he called "lamps") were:

Life   ...Now I call that Living Architecture. There is sensation in every inch of it, and an accommodation to every architectural necessity, with a determined variation in arrangement, which is exactly like the related proportions and provisions in the structure of organic form.[26]

Memory   ...And if indeed there be any profit in our knowledge of the past, or any joy in the thought of being remembered hereafter, which can give strength to present exertion, or patience to present endurance, there are two duties respecting Architecture whose importance it is impossible to overrate: the first, to render the architecture of the day, historical; and, the second, such to preserve, as the most precious of inheritances, that of past ages.[27]

Ruskin's compendium was popularly and ecclesiastically well received – the Protestant Church endorsed the idea that the style and the process of traditional medieval building would promote morality. Also in keeping with Protestant thought, Ruskin held that every man has an innate sense of esthetic truth, directly relating to his spiritual merit. "All men have sense of what is right in this matter, if they would only use and apply this sense; every man knows where and how beauty gives him pleasure, if he would only ask for it when he does so, and not allow it to be forced upon him when he does not want it."[28]

This is an architectural manifestation of Protestant ideals: every man is qualified not only to appreciate design, but to create it. Just as the Protestant Reformation empowered anyone to read scripture and find truth without clergy, Ruskin preached an architectural gospel of the common man, without architects. And, like the Protestant Reformation, the idea caught fire and spread throughout Europe: embraced in France by Eugène Viollet-le-Duc (1814–79), in Italy by Alfredo d'Andrade (1839–1915) and Luca Beltrami (1854–1933), and becoming Europe's epochal architectural style. It was a full-scale movement, soon branded "the Gothic Revival." Ironically, the very rhetoric that exalted the mores of collective design was being trumpeted by individual architects who continued to use modern processes of design and construction. Furthermore, as noted by Alastair Parvin, the focus was myopically on who constructs, rather than the more important question of who pays.[29]

Less than a century later, after the international convulsion of modernism, non-pedigreed design gripped the broader architectural discourse of the 1960s. It became clear that the timeless way of building was not an anachronistic feature of modern man's developmental past – far from it. To this day, communal design continues to trace a vibrant thread through human history and into the 20th century. Notably, English architects Peter and Alison Smithson (1923–2003; 1928–93) spoke into this context, championing ideals similar to Ruskin's. "We in Europe are ready for another architectural ordering that is in a way 'Gothic'; that is, non-compositional, non-theatrical – an ordering we are calling 'conglomerate,'" they wrote. "By this reading...a recovery of sensibilities that had been laid dormant by the overwhelmingly theatrical and graphic character of Italian Renaissance architecture."[30] The Smithsons' work sought to access a climate of artistic production by way of Gothic sensibilities, describing it in the same operative terms that were silenced by Vasari's 1550 campaign for authorship: a return to bottom-up design.

Just as Morris, Ruskin, and Rudofsky before them, architects of the 1960s were beginning to ask, "Why not have the courage, where practical, to let people shape their own environment?" (posed directly by a group of architects and theorists including Reyner Banham, Cedric Price, Peter Hall, and Paul Barker, in their collaborative essay on the theory of "Non-Plan").[31] This simple question impelled a generation of architects and theorists, each offering a twist in flavor or emphasis or design-response. During the 1960s a flood of ideas was brought to the table – varying degrees and means of participation, different boundaries of architect involvement, political or economic definition – but central to all was user empowerment.

One of the earliest examples is Peter and Alison Smithson's open framework for a collectively designed exhibition, *Patio and Pavilion*, shown at "This is Tomorrow" (1956). Decades later, Beatriz Colomina observed that *Patio and Pavilion* was, in a sense, "an ephemeral, un-heroic reply to Le Corbusier's *Pavillon de l'esprit nouveau* of 1925, by which Le Corbusier proposed his *Plan voisin*."[32] As they ceded esthetic control to the practitioners around them, the Smithsons embodied the self-effacing anonymous architect who had been pushed to history's sidelines by the Promethean designer.

N. John Habraken spun the idea slightly differently, suggesting that participatory and flexible design could be achieved by separating structure and infill. He created a "plug and play" system, where the architect delivers hardware (structure) and

sits back to watch as users inject the details of their immediate habitation environment. Yet the idea is more nuanced than
a building-scale cubby-hole, becoming what Japanese expert
on industrial residential design Yositika Utida termed "three-
dimensional urban design."[33] The essence of the concept is the
separation of the individual from the collective, of the part that
changes frequently from what is more stable. This equates with
the distribution of control: control of the unit versus control
of the public whole. The boundary between the two can vary,
as can the identity of the controlling groups – but a balance
between them is the essence of Habraken's idea of "Natural
Relation." It was an elastic and evolutionary response to ideas
of collectivity that also had repercussions in physical, material
space (the framework and contents). In Habraken's model, the
architect provided a system, and inhabitants would appropriate
and respond to it. It is a user-driven interactive architecture that
operates on multiple timescales.[34]

Compelling ideas, but still quite pragmatic. British architect and provocateur Cedric Price (1934–2003) took the idea of
interactivity and sensationalized it. In his hands, architecture
became loud, fun, hip, and constantly evolving – from buildings to proposals for Christmas-tree lights on London's Oxford
Street, Price strove to "enable people to think the unthinkable."
Price understood buildings as venues for interaction, dynamic
scenes that can provoke events and networks, where "delight"
is the operative word, encompassing emotions from creativity to pleasure to shock. In a short essay titled "Follies Can Be
Serious but Not Really Serious: Cedric Price as the Uncrowned
King of Folly," Hans Ulrich Obrist credits the appeal of his
work to "Flexibility, responsiveness, transience, relativity, joy.
Championing these as the principles of urban design, the freeing
of the human within the structure, in opposition to the engrained
doctrine of unyielding, static, constrictive architecture."[35] The

building itself is continuously determined by the users, while the contribution of the architect is to create an infrastructure that anticipates by giving access to (or enforcing) a capability which might not yet have been asked for: Price declared, "like medicine, architecture must move from the curative to the preventative."[36]

He is best known for an unbuilt project, designed with theater director Joan Littlewood (1914–2002), called *The Fun Palace* (1960–61) – a giant framework-machine, schematically coded like a piece of responsive electronic circuitry and driven by the engine of human delight. "Its form and structure, resembling a large shipyard in which enclosures such as theatres, cinemas, restaurants, workshops, rally areas, can be assembled, moved, re-arranged and scrapped continuously."[37] What was most remarkable about Price's work – particularly standing shoulder-to-shoulder with his peers Reyner Banham (1922–88) and François Dallegret, or Archigram – was the lack of interest in graphic visual communication, focusing instead on social criticism and provocation, or posing questions and offering unexpected answers.[38]

A later (also unbuilt) project, *The Generator* (1976), is a more pure expression of Price's cybernetic ideas. The architect was commissioned to create a retreat and activity center for small groups – the perfect brief to apply his concept of an interactive built environment. He devised a system of 150 prefabricated cubes, each 12 x 12 feet, which users could shift and reconfigure. Not only that, but a primitive digital software detected stasis: if the building remained stagnant for too long, it automatically executed *The Boredom Program* to reconfigure the structure and incite (or perturb) users. The architecture itself took an active role as a provocateur, with the aim of enhancing human experience.

For Greek architect Takis Zenetos (1926–77), this suggested a logical continuation: what if experience itself became architecture? Familiar structural forms disappear, becoming, instead, a kind of human-derived network. Zenetos' "Electronic Urbanism" took Price as a starting point – his notions of dynamic planning for the future society – but rather than a sensational architecture of delight, Zenetos placed a sharp focus on contemporary debates within Greek society and economy during the 1960s.[39] "Electronic Urbanism" was directly inspired by science magazines of the time, and proposed a network of overhanging cities as tensile mega-constructions based on a flexible grid that would gradually cover the Earth's surface. Zenetos foresaw the impending telecommunications networks that would lace the globe, and proposed what was, arguably, architecture-as-telecom infrastructure: "The structure of the city and the house of tomorrow will be fleeting almost something fluttering and whenever possible, inmaterial."[40] Similar to Constant Nieuwenhuis' contemporary "New Babylon," Zenetos' imagined future was of a neo-nomadic society inhabiting a dynamic space where links and interactions become more important structure.

Like the Smithsons, Price, and Zenetos, Italian architect Giancarlo de Carlo (1919–2005) sought to reconcile modern life and architecture, working toward desirability and the creation of "scene." "We have not yet built the places 'where it can all happen,'"[41] he wrote, in an essay for Alison Smithson's *Team 10 Primer* (1968), implying that architecture was still ill-fitted to contemporary social patterns. Yet rather than offering an open-ended system, de Carlo scripted dynamism into the architecture itself. "What draws us to Paris is the still-live sense of the city as a collective art-form.... A connection we have now lost. We can rebuild that connection only from the associations of people with places we know to be alive."[42] He vividly described an organic architecture – that is, architecture-as-organism – which would live and breathe with its inhabitants. Rather than expanding additively, it would be organized first at the collective, regional level, and work inward to the basic cell units of individual needs. He saw the distinction between urbanism and architecture as counterproductive and, in blurring the two, worked against the stereotype and endless repetition of modernism. De Carlo's theory did not allow flexibility for the users themselves to change and manipulate the architecture – he believed that such dispersed processes are inefficient and produce poor results. Instead, he proposed intensive research into human patterns, both historic and contemporary, which would provide empirical data to be combined with a biological analogy to create intricate regional systems. De Carlo distilled the idea of a more effective, human, and desirable architecture based on relational infrastructures: users would "design" the architecture simply by their patterns of habitation, which would inform the architect. "Only the assumption of clear ideological positions and the application of rigorously scientific procedure can guarantee a legitimate political and technical framework. Then new objectives can be set and new practical instruments be developed to produce a balanced and stimulating physical environment."[43] Architect became anthropologist, and organic form emerged from his rational analytic processes.

"Methodological investigation on collective forms has seldom been done until very recently," an architect on the other side of the globe had written only three years earlier. "What is needed is not just observation and critical comment, but utilization of the observation to develop strategic tools in making our physical environment."[44] Japanese architect Fumihiko Maki issued this call-to-arms in 1964, sparking a new approach to architectural planning on a regional scale. This was the basic precept driving a coalition of young Japanese radicals, including architects, politicians, designers and economists, who formed the Metabolist movement of the 1960s (discussed in more detail in Chapter 3). As a response to the nation's postwar economic growth and population boom they posited visionary plans for growing, changing, metabolic structures. Architecture must keep up with the pace of society, they argued, and buildings could do so by propagating ad infinitum.

"The force of contemporary urban characteristics makes it impossible to visualize urban form as did Roman military chiefs, or Renaissance architects Sanallo and Michelangelo; nor can we easily perceive a hierarchical order as did the original CIAM theorists [Congrès internationaux d'Architecture Moderne, founded by Le Corbusier in 1928] in the quite recent past. We must now see our urban society as a dynamic field of interrelated forces. It is a set of mutually independent variables in a rapidly expanding infinite series.... Our concern here is not, then, a 'master plan,' but a 'master program,' since the latter term includes a time dimension."[45] Much like an organism, architecture would respond to the pushes and pulls exerted by a matrix of socio-dynamic forces that surround it. Metabolist structures used biological models, achieving dynamism through, for example, spine-and-branch arrangements, or cellularly subdivided megaforms. The architect would establish a system – a master program – that could propagate itself in response to the subsequent social requirements. Maki's early ideas[46] point toward current biological research that investigates the "self-organizing" dynamics of cells and tissue (which can, in turn, provide a concomitant architectural metaphor). As is biology, Metabolist architecture is structure as pattern, aggregation and expansion.

If habitation can be solved with patterns, could a single, robust theory of "pattern language" extend beyond the bounds of architecture? Could applied mathematics arrive at the same flexibility and beauty that Rudofsky documented, that Price and Zenetos shouted for, that de Carlo and Maki researched, and that the Smithsons and Habraken orchestrated?

Christopher Alexander, an iconoclastic mathematician-turned-designer-turned activist based for many years at the University of California, Berkeley, began his work with a seemingly naïve observation – that medieval towns are irregular yet harmonious. With the eye of a mathematician, he interrogated the relationship between guiding regional strictures and the infinite variety that is possible when the architect is free to adapt to a specific site or condition (observations he published in 1979). Once again, an architect had stumbled upon the collective phenomenon:

"There is one timeless way of building. It is a thousand years old, and the same today as it has ever been. The great traditional buildings of the past, the villages and tents and temples in which man feels at home, have always been made by people who were very close to the center of this way. It is not possible to make great buildings, or great towns, beautiful places, places where you feel yourself, places where you feel alive, except by following this way."[47]

Alexander worked to reconcile this human sociability with mathematical patterns, models that would offer a practical generative grammar for building. "These tools allow anyone, and any group of people, to create beautiful, functional, meaningful places.... You can create a living world."[48] A linguistic system for urban networks is based on mathematical models, what Alexander termed the "timeless way of building." Its implementation is through a strictly non-masterplan approach: individual units are subject to local rules, the way humanity has always built.

A living world. A dynamic field of interrelated forces. The city as collective art form. Despite their differences, each of these architectural theories added to the momentum building an exaltation of the anonymous architect. Their final conquest – the last voice to be drowned by the collective shout of participation

– was the unshakable author, the bastion of rhetorical architecture himself: Le Corbusier.

• • • • • • • •

The Swiss built a career atop the edifice that Vasari had begun constructing four hundred years before him. With his authorial hand, proudly gesturing toward a new world and a new spirit, Le Corbusier announced absolute control of society and its design. It is what Haw characterizes as "narcissistic naked aggressive macho individualism."[49] During the process of creating his epochal project, the *Pavillon de l'esprit nouveau*, Le Corbusier was commissioned by industrialist Henri Frugès to design workers' housing in Pessac, southwest France. He brought the same authorial mentality to the project, Les Quartiers Modernes Frugès (completed 1926), and used it as a case study for his "Five Points of Architecture." Le Corbusier described the project as a "laboratory of new domestic, structural and esthetic ideas.... Pessac was built as experimental 'workers' housing.'"[50] It was organized as a standard grid structure – each building designed as an assemblage of universal (almost snap-together) components that fit into the larger plan like pieces of a puzzle.

In its theory and design, the original plan for Cité Frugès appears to be a reconfirmation of Le Corbusier's singular vision, with its pilotis, standardization, and free plan – yet the project's modularity proved to be its Achilles heel. Le Corbusier had created an unexpected alchemy at Pessac: the architectural elements could be configured and reconfigured into any organization...and they were. In the hands of the tenants, the universal components became the key to effacing the architect's deterministic plan – the families of Pessac took full advantage of the flexibility built into their dwellings. Walls were moved, removed or extended, huge (Corbusian) swaths of glass were replaced by sensible little windows with curtains and flower boxes, indoor spaces became outdoor and vice versa. In short, modernism – in all of its white, cubic purity – was decisively shattered. Or rather, it was accessorized.

In elite architectural discourse, Pessac is considered a failure. Thousands of students taking Architectural History 101 courses see it lumped into the lesson plan with St Louis' Pruitt-Igoe (a 1950s Missouri modernist housing project which, ultimately, was dynamited to rubble as the only solution to the violence and squalor for which it became infamous). Pessac's "dynamite" was frilly curtains and Midi-kitsch, but it amounted to the same. Pessac and Pruitt-Igoe are proof that human habitation is at odds with the cold, inhuman sterility possible in architecture. These projects are where a totalizing doctrine went sour.

Yet, this conclusion was questioned by French architect Philippe Boudon, in an incisive 1969 study, *Pessac de Le Corbusier* (published in English in 1972 as *Lived-in Architecture: Le Corbusier's Pessac Revisited*). Boudon reconsidered the project, bringing it into a new, more humanist light. In an exhaustive anthology of photographs, narratives, critical and press responses, interviews, and discussions, he emphasized the agency and significance of Pessac's inhabitants. "The Quartiers Modernes Frugès were not an *architectural failure*," he wrote. "The modifications carried out by the occupants constitute a positive and not a negative consequence of Le Corbusier's original conception. Pessac not only allowed the occupants sufficient latitude to satisfy their needs, by doing so it also helped them to realize what those needs were."[51] Architecture disappeared under a palimpsest of everyday life – could there be value in that very process? After Le Corbusier signed and submitted the plans, the project fermented, and half a century later Boudon uncorked a heady brew of user-empowerment.

The sum total is that Boudon graciously provided the deadliest irony: Pessac wasn't a failure, he said, it was a triumph of collective design! Le Corbusier's method, his manifesto, his very conception of architecture – *that* was a failure. And suddenly Pessac became the final battleground of an ideological war: closed masterpiece or open system?

Critics and theorists fired shots from both camps, but Boudon's *Pessac Revisited* was effectively the final nail in the clean, white coffin of authorial design. Ada Louise Huxtable (1921–2013) reexamined Les Quartiers Modernes Frugès and added her voice to the cacophony, grafting Le Corbusier's iconic words back onto the project: "Le Corbusier once said, in a statement usually turned against him, 'You know, it is always life that is right and the architect who is wrong.' This was not a confession of error. It was the recognition of the validity of process over the sanctity of ideology. Few architects are capable of making that observation, because it speaks not to some fixed ideal, but to the complexity and incompleteness of architecture, to how life and art accommodate to each other. And that is what Pessac is really about."[52] Huxtable summarized her impression, "I have been to Pessac to see the future and contrary to popular belief and the conventional wisdom, it works." A compelling proof of non-pedigreed architecture.

The families of Pessac had dealt a deadly blow of kitsch to Le Corbusier's pure architecture, and when critics such as Boudon and Huxtable spun the carnage in a positive light they achieved nothing short of the final dismantlement of the ideology that Le Corbusier represented. The Swiss was dead, but he had created something spectacular and unexpected with the Cité Frugès. Ultimately, "there is no sense of 'the architect's will imposed,' or of an unyielding, authoritarian design. The houses rolled with the punches"[53] – a fine result of interactive alchemy and bold inhabitants, but the question that remained was whether such flexibility could be designed from the beginning. Could the dream of participatory architecture ever blossom into a functional operational model, as had authorial design?

The simple answer is: no. Even today, almost fifty years later, it doesn't seem so. That energy contained in the white-hot ideas of collective design that razed modernism, that had architects and theorists from Price to de Carlo buzzing, had all but fizzled out. The convivial Gothic mentality, the interactive *Fun Palace*, the generative "pattern languages"...why didn't it all come true?

3
·······

Why It Did Not Work: A Horse Designed by Committee

Participation will create chaos.

Christopher Alexander, *The Oregon Experiment*, 1975[1]

Chemical plants. Industrial parks. Landfills and toxic waste containment facilities. Highways. Youth Hostels. Prisons. Nuclear, coal, and natural gas power plants. We are familiar with – and probably guilty of – the NIMBY mentality: Not In My Back Yard.

The sentiment is nothing new – there is evidence of it long before radiation and cellphone towers. Its proto-form was probably NIMT (Not In My Tree) or NIMC (Not In My Cave), but our story begins with NIMEY (Not In My Estate Yard). The year is 1833, and the estate in question is Clement Clarke Moore's Chelsea, on the western edge of Manhattan Island. The City of New York had recently passed the Commissioner's Plan of 1811, which proposed a new Ninth Avenue running directly through Chelsea. After unsuccessfully protesting against the urbanization of his land, Moore was considering an attractive offer of forty thousand dollars for the whole estate. At the last minute, James Wells (the founder of the United States' first real estate office) convinced him to retain ownership of the land and to parcel it out into individual development lots. By 1835, Wells had drawn a preliminary street plan for the newly incorporated area and become an investor himself, purchasing an office at 191 Ninth Avenue. Wells' proposal was a vision of participatory development – as the land was sold to individual owners, it would be built up collectively into a thriving town. The process would not be entirely organic – it was, after all, privately owned land, and "all kinds of Nuisances will be prohibited,"[2] Moore reasoned. To guide Chelsea's growth, he and Wells established strict regulations on future construction (essentially, proto-zoning) and he reserved the right to approve or deny any project.

Not strict enough, it seems. By 1845, a mere five years after the land was parceled out, several disgruntled owners complained to Moore for approving the construction of "small unsightly frame buildings," near their own lots. The worst blight of all, they said, "to cap the climax of injustice,"[3] was a carpenter's shop on Ninth Avenue. A letter addressed to Moore and Wells stated that the shop "materially depress[ed] the value of all property in the immediate neighborhood," and constituted an "express violation of your own assurances to us."[4] Communal design had worked perfectly, until too many incompatible voices and ideas came to the table, leaving only a single piece of common ground: a great collective shout of "Not In My Back Yard!"

• • • • • • • •

The wisdom of the crowd, the challenge of herding cats, and the NIMBY mentality that locks it all into stalemate – in any collaborative project, the difficulty is to maximize participation while maintaining a clear order and a unified focus. With his "Pattern Language," Christopher Alexander offered a model of participatory design, showing that what he called "the timeless way of building" can yield powerful results. And what better place to test his theory than a thriving community of bright, engaged intellectuals who cared about their physical environment?

This was the kernel of The Oregon Experiment, described in an eponymous book.[5] During the 1960s and '70s, the University of Oregon campus in Eugene, Oregon, was crackling with activist energy. Student groups were publicly engaged with political affairs at national and international levels, including the United States' military draft, human rights in Nepal, and policy regarding the Vietnam War – as well as such local matters as the destruction of a 19th-century cemetery, Oregon-based industrial logging, and Reserve Officers' Training Corps involvement at the university. The critical student body also railed against the campus itself: a scattering of World War II-era Brutalist housing blocks that they decried as a concrete entrenchment of archaic pedagogy and social views. Students protested against the structures of the university, both physical and ideological, and called for an administration that took into account their views and provided a hospitable environment.

Their champion was Christopher Alexander: that rare kind of architect who – given the commission to develop a masterplan – would choose not to design buildings, but a mathematical, grammatical design language. Alexander worked to create a system that could integrate the users (specifically the disgruntled and active student population) with planners, designers, and administrators. The key was a language based on a non-technical and non-specialist vocabulary of design principles. It wasn't mathematics, exactly – it was a functional tool for discussion. This new methodology would "define a pattern as any general planning principle which states a clear problem that may occur repeatedly in the environment, states the range of contexts in which this problem will occur, and gives the general features required by all buildings or plans which will solve this problem."[6] In effect, Alexander was offering a radical new approach to designing best-fit yet cohesive environments for a large community of stakeholders, one that would allow decisions to be made continuously by the entire group, rather than be guided by a strict, original, and singular masterplan. His "pattern language" would be the flexible glue that held an evolving campus-scale project together.

"But of course, in order to create order, not chaos, people must have some shared principles. Nothing would be worse than an environment in which each square foot was designed according to entirely different principles. This would be chaos indeed.

In our proposal, this problem is solved by the use of the shared 'patterns'.... These patterns give the users a solid base for their design decisions. Each person and group of people will be able to make unique places, but always within the morphological framework created by the patterns."[7] As the saying goes, a camel is a horse designed by committee,[8] and Alexander's entire system existed to mediate and strike a balance between innovation and chaos. He built-in protection against the latter, structuring his pattern language to prevent disorder, and taking for granted a motive force of engaged students, vibrant discussion, collaboration, and participation.

Alexander had wagered on the wrong cards. The fatal flaw of the project – one that Alexander did not anticipate, despite the sophistication of his pattern language – was the difficulty of attracting stakeholders to the actual, nitty-gritty, raise-your-hand-and-vote process of making decisions. His linguistic system worked so hard to make a seamless and flexible participatory process that it did not account for student apathy. Soon it became clear that the only way to arrive at a conclusion in campus planning was to address the issue in a targeted group, meaning that vast numbers of stakeholders might never hear about a decision, let alone weigh in on it – finally rendering the participatory system irrelevant. With each year that passed sans broader student input, Alexander's pattern language withered.

In 1994, architecture critic Greg Bryant returned to The Oregon Experiment, observing that, "the democratic safeguards, the annual reviews and diagnoses, have disappeared. Campus planners blame this on a lack of resources, but these events could be organized by faculty and students. Only a handful of people are now involved in what's left of the process. Some find it empowering, but others quickly find its limits."[9] The majority of the student body had no idea that the university was carrying out a planning experiment. Alexander had built safeguards of community control into his pattern language to protect against the undue influence of bureaucracy, administrative power and financial leverage. Arguably, this was a flexible and evolving framework, and the system itself could have generated that shift – as Giancarlo de Carlo had written decades earlier: "collective participation introduces a plurality of objectives and actions whose outcomes cannot be foreseen..."[10] one of which might turn out to be the self-destruction of the system itself. But the net result was that the original vision of energetic community participation had been lost. The only thing against which Alexander could not protect was indifference, and at the outset of the project – on a campus buzzing with pent-up energy – it would not have seemed necessary. In his revisitation of The Oregon Experiment, Bryant wrote that the students "are apathetic...because no one asks them anything. The administration does not generally give to the campus community the political power to make decisions."[11]

After two decades, the Oregon Experiment was either dead or had mutated into the ideological antithesis of its original intention. Christopher Alexander returned to the task of integrating users and balancing conflicting agendas in a later book – titled nothing less than *The Nature of Order Book Three*[12] – in which he considered the idea from the perspective of builders and administrators. Particularly in the context of large-scale projects, he concluded that the process is "a political and administrative nightmare."[13] Democracy could result in either bland stalemate or fruitless chaos – The Oregon Experiment produced a lowest common denominator, and the only recourse was to continue the university's bureaucratic status quo. In a sense, the outcome was unsurprising. "No wonder participation by users is so often refused by administrators – in buildings *and* in towns,"[14] wrote Alexander. With his Oregon Experiment, he had squared off against a monumental challenge, and it had proven impossible.

Could there be a solution to both apathy and anarchy? The idea of The Oregon Experiment had been good, thought architects, but the execution failed. This central question sparked a burgeoning discussion during the 1970s, nowhere as energetically as the Massachusetts Institute of Technology (MIT) campus, where lines blurred between computer science and architecture, then as now. Eager talk of computing, programming, machines, and generative code was flying thick in the air, and architects were breathing deeply. Among the most vocal was Nicholas Negroponte, who led the MIT Soft Architecture Machine Group to propose methods for schematizing participation, essentially turning it into software. A new kind of design emerged, based on science. American academic and theorist Herbert A. Simon (1916–2001) published *The Sciences of the Artificial* in 1969, in which he described this new formula as "a body of intellectually tough, analytic, partly formalizable, partly empirical, teachable doctrine about the design process."[15] The goal was a non-chaotic system with categorically guaranteed user input for the maximum efficiency of user-derived output.

Moving beyond the barn-raising mentality, a new, complex theory of collaboration was emerging from breakthrough technologies. In 1965, British designer L. Bruce Archer (1922–2005) – one of the pioneers of design as an academic discipline – summarized the crystallizing field: "The most fundamental challenge to conventional ideas on design has been the growing advocacy of systematic methods of problem solving, borrowed from computer techniques and management theory, for the assessment of design problems and the development of design solutions."[16] The roots of this new design methodology had been sewn during World War II, when an unprecedented amount of data – including governance, finance, personnel, tactics, propaganda, and nutrition, to name but a few – generated by the war effort required what became known as a new "systems thinking" paradigm. In the broadest sense, this was a new science relating to the exchange of knowledge between nodes of a cybernetic system, and its insights could be applied to any discipline or specific challenge. Working in terms of interrelated networks of contingencies soon spread to architecture, and was the subject of several books, design initiatives, and academic conferences.[17]

In the case of architecture, systematizing collaborative design seemed to be a surefire solution, bolstered by new technologies for computation. As the field was developed, however, the complexity of computational methods increased exponentially, and the discourse surrounding methodical collaboration soon became so esoteric and difficult to implement that it was irrelevant to anyone but the designer himself (and perhaps abstruse even to him). These new methods had become either a labyrinthine mechanism that ultimately dissuaded engagement, or a dumbed-down apparatus of compromise. UC Berkeley professors of design Horst Rittel (1930–90) and Melvin Webber (1920–2006) framed it as a "wicked problem"[18] in their 1973 essay "Dilemmas in a General Theory of Planning."[19] The phrase indicates, specifically, that systematic social design is difficult or impossible ("wicked"), due to shifting requirements and interdependencies that cause any given solution to result in additional problems. "It had to be acknowledged," they determined, "that there had been a lack of success in the application of "scientific" methods to design."[20] Often, such methods yielded nothing but a recognition of the lowest common denominator – arriving at a "satisfactory" solution that does the least harm to the greatest number, rather than solving difficult problems. And if not, participation was strictly on the designer's terms. A 2005 study titled *Architecture and Participation* concluded that: "the strong feeling is that participation, or rather pseudo-participation, is being used as a socially acceptable shield behind which the authors can develop their technically-determined ideologies,"[21] (ironically, the study was group-authored).

The dream of collaboration and participation was a consummate failure in both cases – the damning apathy of Alexander's Oregon Experiment, and the snowballing complexity of systematic design theories by computer scientists. Yet, as the authors of *Architecture and Participation* suggest, nominally cooperative projects, in any bastardized form, nonetheless continue to be a useful tool for architects and administrators alike. Proof is in the mark that Christopher Alexander left on the University of Oregon: the planning principles of pattern language are ostensibly still in place today, forty years later...but only as a veneer for bureaucratic decision-making. The university has institutionalized pseudo-participation, to mild – if not completely irrelevant – ends.

An entirely sanitized form of collaboration keeps the board happy and keeps the students happy. In his book *Community Participation Methods in Design and Planning* (1999), Henry Sanoff qualified this practice. "Pseudo-participation was categorized as (1) Domestication: this involves informing, therapy, and manipulation, or (2) Assistencialism: this involves placation and consultation."[22] A select few have control, and the majority is complicit: feeling involved, but without serious responsibilities. The word "participation" is clearly a powerful selling tool, regardless of its problematic feasibility, and adds the weight of democratic validation to any planning process. In reference to The Oregon Experiment, Bryant wrote, "This self-deception, not coincidentally, gives the administration unilateral control with a useful gloss of community responsibility."[23] Essentially, the rhetoric of participation is useful, but participation itself is not – and so collaboration fades into irrelevance as it boils down to the same old top-down politics.

It satisfies institutional boards, but true participation is deeply unpalatable for architects. N. John Habraken tells an anecdote of his work during the 1960s, in the context of a "rhetoric of participation" – which, he found, was ultimately an attempt by the professional architect to stay in control. Empowered designers declared themselves ready to listen to the people but jealously guarded the bottom-line design decisions. "We rejected that notion, arguing that the user should not participate in the professional controlled game but should get control of his own," explains Habraken. "The result was that we were not trusted and got called technocrats because we pointed out the material potential of our proposal. Even Giancarlo de Carlo finally blurted out that in housing projects the house unit's floor plan could only be decided by an architect. The case of user control still needs to be made in professional circles...."[24]

Habraken's response was to create a hybrid system in which various arenas of control versus user participation exist side-by-side – or rather, bottom-up design grows to inhabit and animate the cells of a larger framework. He developed a "natural relation" theory of mass housing based on a structure-infill system that worked in tandem with users, like a beehive's honey-to-honeycomb structure. The power of Habraken's model is that the house unit – or work unit or any minimum material element of the built environment – corresponds directly with the smallest social unit in a society. By allowing it to be individually controlled, it becomes, once again, a living cell in the organic built environment. A housing project can be any size – the framework is extensible – yet it maintains its fine-grained relationship to inhabitants as it dynamically changes over time.[25] Habraken developed his theory of separating support and infill in a 1961 book *Supports: an Alternative to Mass Housing*, making a compelling case for buildings acquiring the scale and lifespan of cities. Whether Marxist or capitalist (Habraken has been called both), he boldly announced that such a separation in architecture is "inevitable,"[26] a feature of the autonomous built environment.

Postwar Japan was also faced with the challenge of providing mass housing, and arrived at a similarly modular conclusion. The specific context called for a new model of habitation befitting a society that, in its own eyes, was poised to grow exponentially – not only in terms of population, but also economically, culturally, and in global positioning. With this context as a motive force, a group of young architects, designers, and politicians coalesced around the idea of "metabolic" architecture: an entirely new system that would expand, change, and adapt to Japan's explosive growth, maximizing the limited resource of physical space on the main island of Honshu.

The work of the Metabolists, as they came to be known, was propelled by the World Design Conference (WoDeCo) hosted by Japan in 1960. With the entire world as their audience, the Metabolists submitted a radical manifesto for the future, *METABOLISM 1960: Proposals for a New Urbanism*. During the following ten years, the group generated a prolific body of otherworldly habitation-concepts – although very few were ever built. Projects ranged in scale from individual buildings to sweeping megacities, seeking to multiply physical space by reaching up into the air, spreading out across the surface of the ocean, or plunging down to its farthest depths. Technology was central, and across the Metabolist movement its application ranged from towering helixes to extensive A-frames, to vast floating webs. The architecture most often echoed biological models, allowing for growth based on spine-and-branch organization, or replicating cellular-vascular structures. It was as if Habraken's ideas for a natural order were put into electric, churning motion: the individual habitation cell became an infinitely replicable, propagating biological unit, driving the architect's ego to colossal scale.

Taking the traditional Japanese village as a starting point for his theoretical work, Metabolist founding member Fumihiko Maki presented a short essay titled *Investigations in Collective Form* (1964).[27] In it, he suggested the term "megastructure" to represent any building-as-ecosystem that folds vernacular social organization into a single structure; a man-made feature of the geological and cultural landscape. The example Maki held as a paragon of megastructure was the 1960 *Project for 25,000*, designed by Kenzo Tange (1913–2005) in conjunction with the MIT School of Architecture and Planning. To accommodate a population of twenty-five thousand, the housing block was proposed as two linear buildings of tremendous scale stretching out into Boston Harbor; each composed of a fixed framework – the bones – and autonomous, rapidly interchangeable functional units – the cells. The buildings would be connected to each other and to the land by major highways, asserting the gargantuan scale and technological vision of the scheme.

These are all theoretical proposals – however, a handful of realized buildings exists. The Nakagin Capsule Tower (1972), designed by Kisho Kurokawa (1934–2007), is located in central Tokyo and is in active use as an apartment building. It is conceived as a central spine (holding utilities and circulation), into which individual housing pods can be plugged and rearranged. Infinite combinations of pods and connections between them would allow for the creation of larger or smaller spaces; in theory, these can respond dynamically to the needs of larger or smaller families. Yet just as the Capsule Tower distills Metabolist ideas, it also reveals a deep conceptual frailty: since the building's completion in 1972, not a single pod has been shifted or combined.

The common features of Metabolist architecture were a certain dynamism and a scale far beyond what humans had ever previously proposed. And therein lay the problem. For all of the interchangeable potential and visionary structural innovation, these buildings were inhuman. In his 1964 essay, Maki was already critical of the tendency toward "structural virtuosity at the expense of human scale and human functional needs," and the fallibility of the structure-infill system itself, observing that "if the megaform becomes rapidly obsolete, as well it might... it will be a great weight about the neck of urban society."[28] He envisioned a dystopian future landscape littered with gargantuan skeletons of disused megastructures.

Their proposals were visionary, solutions were grand, but the fundamental inhumanity of mutability and megastructure – let alone the economic and political barriers to implementing such vast urban projects – caused the Metabolist movement to flash out of existence just as suddenly as it had begun.

Yet the idea of megastructure persisted. During the 1970s the model of a honeycomb structure filled with cells for habitation continued to veer toward the colossal and dissociate from human proportion. Rather than following the progression of earlier so-called participatory architecture – becoming largely irrelevant, or theoretical beyond implementation – these projects were uncompromisingly severe in both their conception and their appearance. They worked with the same scale and concept as Metabolism, but their expression was starkly brutal: crystalline rather than organic. Corviale (1972), a housing project on the outskirts of Rome, aggressively followed in the tradition of Le Corbusier's concept of the "Unité d'habitation" (housing unit). Designed to be a comprehensive city-in-a-box, it offered a space for every social function – from schools to shops to chapels – within a single massive structure. The intent behind Corviale was to alleviate congestion in the ancient Roman city center by creating an autonomous and self-supporting block of 1,200 apartments some fifteen kilometers away from the downtown area. Corviale was collaboratively designed by a team of five Italian architects: Frederick Gorio, Piero Maria Lugli

(1923–2008), Giulio Sterbini (1912–87) and Michele Valori (1923–79), coordinated by Mario Fiorentino (1918–82).

As dictated by the architects, Corviale took the form of two parallel and mirroring buildings, each nine stories tall and a full kilometer long, earning it the nickname "giant serpent." A narrow cleft between the two halves was interspersed with open public areas and flanked by long interior corridors that unified the length of the building, providing a means of circulation. Individual housing units were systematically and densely packed throughout, with the fourth floor reserved as an interior shopping street.

In 1982, only months after the structure opened (construction had not been finished, and is still not complete to this day), Corviale was already illegally occupied. More than seven hundred families were squatting in the disused public areas and vacant storefronts of the fourth-floor commercial district – a street now called the "flying favela."[29] It had been impossible to attract business to the illogically placed shopping arcade, and the partitioned shops became perfect (free) apartments for two, even three families – far more people than these spaces would have warranted had they even been meant for habitation. In lieu of retail, a much more thriving economy – narcotics, prostitution and other illegal activity – developed throughout the building. Conditions were dismally oppressive for inhabitants, who fought for what little light and private space the building offered. Designed with the vision of bringing natural sunlight down into an attractive and bustling pedestrian boulevard, the interior fissure was instead a sheer vertical face that dwarfed human proportion. From the exterior, Corviale was a stark, brutal gash across the Roman countryside and, within its walls, the project quickly became a festering beehive of human habitation. The same year he saw Corviale inhabited, the chief architect, Mario Fiorentino, died of a heart attack – though the pervasive rumor is that he committed suicide (a tale that proves the public's opinion).

However horrifying, Corviale was not the only built attempt at megastructure during this time; it seems that a participatory mentality necessarily led to the same conclusion in many simultaneous instances around the world. Peter and Alison Smithson responded to a similar brief in a similar context – a housing block on the outskirts of London – and devised a structure that echoed both Corviale and the Boston Harbor project. Like them, Robin Hood Gardens, as it was called (completed 1972), was split into two linear concrete buildings, cupping public space between them. Like them, Robin Hood Gardens contained internal circulation paths (what the Smithsons called "streets in the sky"[30]) that were meant to become vibrant thoroughfares, a focal point of the building that sought to foster a thriving community within a hermetic project.

It was envisioned as a new housing typology, one that would demonstrate new analogues for elements of the traditional city – the house, the street, the neighborhood. With changes in modern transportation, for example, would come a new definition of "street" – one without cars, yet nonetheless providing the age-old benefits of views, circulation, light, and air.

Far from new paradigms, Robin Hood Gardens reaped nothing but accusations of "inhumane planning" and a "social cesspool;"[31] as low construction quality became increasingly apparent, crime and squalor rose. Complaints ranged from trash accumulation and leaking roofs to overcrowded flats housing multiple families. Within only a few years of its completion in 1972, tenants had already begun to advocate the building's destruction – met by an equal and opposite preservationist campaign from city government (loathe, as they were, to invest in alternatives).

"People live in Robin Hood Gardens, like they live in a prison," said resident Charles Alison. "You could be walking along and all of a sudden you find something has hit you – an egg, a stone, a drink or cup thrown from the top." Fellow resident Obadiah Chambers said: "They should pull it down, without a doubt. They would not be pulling my home down because I don't call it a home."[32]

Even Peter Smithson, when asked about the work in a 1990s interview, could not endorse Robin Hood Gardens. "In other places you see doors painted and pot plants outside houses, the minor arts of occupation, which keep the place alive. In Robin Hood you don't see this because if someone were to put anything out, people would break it.... The week it opened, people would shit in the lifts."[33]

After numerous campaigns for the destruction and replacement of Robin Hood Gardens, the tenants – themselves its most outspoken critics – have finally made their voices heard. In April of 2013, after forty-one years of poor conditions (in what many described as a near-uninhabitable building), the process of demolition began.

● ● ● ● ● ● ● ●

Architects return, again and again, to participatory design – or rather, the rhetoric of participation is hung as an accessory on many kinds of architectural project. Yet collaboration appears to be a treacherous foundation for the planning process, yielding a spectrum of results from apathy to anarchy.

That isn't to say architecture is without collective action. Far from it – the built environment is a powerful catalyst of the unified public. The Metabolists were a huge media success, far beyond what their built *oeuvre* would suggest. WoDeCo put the group in the global spotlight. Kenzo Tange appeared on Japan's national television network, NHK,[34] to present his ideas; and images of the Osaka World Expo – the last great Metabolist project, in 1970 – captivated audiences across the globe. The Metabolists charmed designers and non-designers alike with powerful visions of the future, garnering Japanese and international support.

In the case of Robin Hood Gardens (much to the chagrin of the architects) the most vibrant participation happened after the building had been completed and residents had moved in – taking shape as a vocal campaign for demolition. The future of the housing project was hotly contested in an evolving succession of media: letters, press, blogs, and finally Facebook and social media. Exposés showed squalor, while preservationists proudly cited Architecture (with a capital A), and cynics called it a moot point. The net result was dissatisfaction, and it quickly grew to become a full-scale movement for demolition.

In 2013, as bulldozers finally rolled onto the site, its failure was confirmed...but could Robin Hood Gardens show the glimmer of a new paradigm? After four decades of contention, it was finally the limitless and instantaneous connectivity of digital networks that tipped the balance, catalyzing residents' engagement with each other and with decision makers. Physical networks of proximity – which had been essentially the same for decades at Robin Hood Gardens – were not as powerful as the energetic publics of virtual space. Could a new networked era yet provide connective tools to enact a timeless paradigm for participation?

4

....

Learning From the Network: New Paradigms for Participation in the Digital World

How shall the new environment be programmed now that we have become so involved with each other, now that all of us have become the unwitting work force for social change? What's that buzzzzzzzzzzzzzzzzzzzzzzzzing?

Marshall McLuhan, *The Medium is the Massage*, 1967[1]

On August 26, 1991, a twenty-one-year-old comp-sci student at the University of Helsinki sat in front of his home computer, wearing a bathrobe. For about five months, he had spent his free time toying with an alternative to Minix, an education-oriented operating system. With the code nearing completion, he typed a short message into an online forum to ask for casual feedback: "I'm doing a (free) operating system (just a hobby, won't be big and professional like gnu) for 386(486) AT clones."[2]

His name was Linus Torvalds, and he had just created the "kernel" of an operating system (the system software that runs a computer) – a seed that would grow into the paradigm-shifting Linux platform, and leave an indelible mark on the means and the ends of software production. As a student, Torvalds had simply been developing a tool for his own personal use, to facilitate access to the school's large Unix servers, but as it progressed, he quickly realized that he had created the foundations of something larger. By the end of the summer he had uploaded it onto the school's FTP server to ease broader distribution and development – initially under the name Freax (although, unbeknown to Torvalds, a friend of his invoked network administrator privilege and renamed it Linux).

In 1992, as it gained steam at the university, the source code for the operating system was made public under the GNU General Public License, free to be changed, augmented, and developed by anyone with a computer and Internet access. To date, hundreds of thousands of suggested changes have been sent to "maintainers" – Torvalds among them – to be implemented in the main Linux kernel. This piece of software has been built by a completely open and distributed team of developers....

And it works.

Torvalds adamantly believes that "open-source is the only right way to do software,"[3] a stance that is continually proven by Linux' robust performance in both personal and commercial applications. Many banks today, for example, use Linux for security reasons, and developers prefer it for its flexibility.[4] It is an entirely new conception of design, what academic and sociologist Richard Sennett calls "public craft."[5] With the staggering momentum of programmers worldwide pushing it forward, Linux has evolved in ways that proprietary software could never have done. It stands as a testament to the heterogeneous entities that assembled it – a million vibrant particles, amateur and adept, with a tangle of agendas and interests. The chemistry of a diffuse networked intelligence is a tremendous force of innovation and disruption, on a scale that humans have never worked before.

Torvalds remains involved in the project as a grandfather, of sorts, and embraces the dizzying heterogeneity of Linux. In his view, the maelstrom of voices and ideas and disagreements and innovations only serves to strengthen the final product. "To me, the discussion would be about how to work together despite these kinds of cultural differences, not about 'how do we make everybody nice and sing songs around the campfire?'."[6] Torvalds, the self-proclaimed "King of Geeks" envisioned Linux as the ultimate capitulation of top-down corporate software development. Never one to miss an opportunity for thumbing his nose at corporate culture, Torvalds – to this day – asserts his right to not wear a tie, to code from his bedroom and wear a bathrobe. "Really, I'm not out to destroy Microsoft. That will just be a completely unintentional side effect."[7]

• • • • • • • •

Without rehearsing the threadbare rhetorical sparring between collectivism, communism and capitalism, it is still possible to delve into a larger discourse of human social systems. The work of Benjamin Franklin (1706–90) – one of the fathers of a capitalist nation – expressly engaged this tension. In addition to his role in writing and signing all four of the founding documents of the United States,[8] Franklin was an insatiable creator; his *oeuvre* included bifocals, swim fins, charting and explaining Atlantic Ocean currents, the urinary catheter, and the Franklin Stove... yet he held not a single patent. In today's world, where everything from intellectual property to individual threads on a screw merits a patent, it is unthinkable that such a prolific inventor would loosen his grip on proprietary ideas. In the case of the stove – a dramatic and marketable improvement on existing technology – Franklin was explicitly offered a patent. He wrote, in his autobiography, "Gov'r. Thomas was so pleas'd with the construction of this stove...that he offered to give me a patent for the sole vending of them for a term of years; but I declin'd it."[9] The only explanation that Franklin offered was one of pure altruism. Ideas, he thought, should be shared, tested and proved, for the benefit of whoever would use them. "As we enjoy great advantages from the inventions of others, we should be glad of an opportunity to serve others by any invention of ours; and this we should do freely and generously."[10]

Benjamin Franklin had adopted a truly open mentality: rather than a top-down implementation of collaborative methods, he was more interested in putting the product, idea, or process directly into the hands of the public. He was confident that humanity would be best served by the free and open ownership of his ideas, and happily allowed the public to actively change and augment them. To this end, he published his work in pamphlets, general magazines, and leaflets – most notably the *Pennsylvania Gazette* and *Poor Richard's Almanac* – using his own printing shop. In 1731, he even opened the United States' first circulating library, all the better to share knowledge widely.

The shared-information ecology that Franklin imagined and worked to create was defined by means of communication – whether an almanac, town library or periodical. Throughout the history of human settlement, from governance to religious ritual to shared child-rearing, the village or town has been a standard unit of social collective experience, its size defined by the extents of direct human contact. Even before these social units emerged, the invention and implementation of cultural products – language, cooking or architecture – have always advanced slowly, over centuries, in the context of individual communities. The exchange of knowledge within the collective is activated by the invisible infrastructures of the relational social unit. Human traditions and relationships are the means, not only to transmit information, but also to expand, augment, and contextualize it. It is an evolutionary process, driven by face-to-face human action and interaction as a form of natural selection.

And then suddenly, at the turn of the 20th century, for the first time since the printing press, a new means of communication wildly skewed the neighborhood-metric by orders of magnitude: wireless radio. The elements of the village – whether social or functional – took on new reactive properties as they amplified explosively. Canadian social media theorist Marshall McLuhan (1911–80) described this new human connective paradigm as a "global village"[11] – an entire planet talking as if neighbors, suddenly given the tools to access each other's ideas. Humanity had become ubiquitously and a-spatially connected. Yet it was different from traditional village communication in one crucial way: information was conveyed unilaterally. Radio is either received or broadcast – it is not conversational.

The term "global village" was perhaps inspired by a tradition of the Roman Catholic Church, *Urbi et Orbi* (the city and the globe). This is the name of the Pope's annual Easter and Christmas addresses to Rome and to the church body around the world, and – in the same way – it is monologue rather than dialogue. As he speaks directly to the audience, time and space collapse: individual nodes of the global Catholic network become instantaneously connected by his words.

McLuhan's global village, however, does not point toward cohesiveness within the Catholic church – far from it – he qualified the term with its inherent tensions. "The more you create village conditions, the more discontinuity and division and diversity. The Global Village absolutely insures maximal disagreement on all points. It never occurred to me that uniformity and tranquility were the properties of the global village. It has more spite and envy. The spaces and times are pulled out from between people. A world in which people encounter each other in depth all the time. The tribal-global village is far more divisive – full of fighting – than any nationalism ever was. Village is fission, not fusion, in depth all the time."[12] Even if, elsewhere in his work, McLuhan suggests a more polyphonic outcome, the global village often defaults to a forum for shouting – as if a planet filled with megaphones.

The emerging networked condition of the Internet era is markedly different. It brings together conflicting ideas and ideals, but most importantly, it is a conversation. It returns to the original, age-old village metric. The Internet allows a two-way exchange of ideas, not just a broadcast, and this cocktail of discord and collectivism can be remarkably productive, as proven by open-source software. Linus Torvalds embraced the cacophony generated by Linux, believing that ultimately it enriches the final product. Today, the same energy that yielded vernacular architecture everywhere, Gothic cathedrals in

Europe, and barns in rural North America is projected beyond the face-to-face, local scale and into the vast global expanse of the Internet.

The broad term "Internet" implies more than just the early network of computers developed through the US military's project ARPA-net during the 1960s and '70s. The social platform that grew on top of that infrastructure – essentially, a means of easily accessing information on the Internet – came to be known as the World Wide Web. The Web allowed for "the creation of new links and new material by readers, [so that] authorship becomes universal" – according to its credited inventor Tim Berners-Lee. Those readers-as-authors were the key to success – Berners-Lee chose to distribute the idea freely, without royalties, as a completely open innovation, so that anyone and everyone could partake in the platform and contribute to it. The rest is history. In 2012 Berners-Lee was officially recognized as the "Inventor of the World Wide Web" during the summer Olympics Opening Ceremony in London. From the stage, he Tweeted "This is for everyone,"[13] – a message not only to the eighty thousand people in attendance, but blasted across the globe, through the Internet itself.

As it developed, the World Wide Web became a reflexive test-bed and workshop for a new kind of participatory design. The public it enabled autopoeitically came into being – people used the Internet to create the Internet (an artifact of simultaneous communication and substance). It was a phenomenon of connectivity, as McLuhan presciently observed: "The whole tendency of modern communication... is toward participation in a process, rather than apprehension of concepts."[14] Because it is entirely open-ended, with no hierarchical structure save that of its constituent parts, the Internet remains a "Wild West" of unbridled potential (and also, ironically, enclaves of control). Anyone and everyone can communicate, collaborate, create content or platforms and connect them to any other. "The number of such creations, circulations, and borrowings has exploded," observed cultural theorist Christopher Kelty, "and the tools of knowledge creation and circulation (software and networks) have also become more and more pervasively available.... All of these concerns amount to a 'reorientation of knowledge and power.'"[15]

The most potent consequence of this reorientation, as far as Kelty is concerned, is Free Software – digital content that is unambiguously free of both cost and ownership. The term "Free Software" designates a program whose source code (its constituent DNA) is publically available for addition, mutation, and implementation. The most remarkable quality of Free Software is not its potential for technical innovations – although those are plenty – but its dependence upon an active network of people who contribute enthusiastically. The key thing is that it is neither entirely altruistic nor entirely self-interested. As it flies in the face of conventional market norms, open sourcing becomes, on the one hand, an economy of reputation, and on the other, simple pragmatism (Torvalds famously coined the quip, be lazy like a fox). Altruism aside, it is simply inefficient to reinvent the wheel every time you want to design anything, and too expensive to do all the testing and R&D that the crowd will do.[16] Collective production is a kind of non-monetary economy animated by transactions between amateurs and paid professionals, all choosing to share their end product.

Linux is perhaps the best example. Driven by an alchemy of motives, coders worldwide download, tinker with, improve, and re-submit code to Linux: estimates put the number of users well into the tens of millions. As of 2011, those users have written fifteen million lines of code, which to develop by traditional proprietary (read: Microsoft-ian) methods would cost an estimated three billion dollars. Open-sharing communities, it seems, can dramatically outperform organizations with standard development methods.

Major corporations have not remained blind to the groundswell of open-source design. Netscape was one of the first companies to realize the possibility of harnessing the prodigious creative power of the world at large and responded with an unprecedented business decision. In 1998, the company released the source code for Netscape Communicator 5.0 to the public, with the hope of accelerating its development and broadening its operational potential. "By giving away the source code for future versions, we can ignite the creative energies of the entire Net community and fuel unprecedented levels of innovation in the browser market," announced CEO Jim Barksdale. "Our customers can benefit from world-class technology advancements; the development community gains access to a whole new market opportunity; and Netscape's core businesses benefit from the proliferation of the market-leading client software."[17] The result is a piece of software we now know as Mozilla Firefox, but the most significant repercussion of Netscape's decision was the explosion of "open source" as a concept onto the global stage in 1999: the phrase appeared on the cover of *Forbes* magazine, the Free Software Foundation was established, and open sourcing became the hot topic of political, economic, legal, and (of course) technological debate and practice.

It became obvious during the media boom that Free Software is not only a productive collaboration model, but also a forceful political statement. It has come to represent an ethical and social position on questions of copyright and ownership, surveillance, transnational corporations, and overarching systems of governance. Free Software has become analogous to free speech, free press, assembly, and petition: it is a means not only to express a political stance, but also to enact it. As Kelty said, it is "a reorientation of knowledge and power."[18]

Put simply, open-source software has achieved an unprecedented level of technological sophistication through communal design, and it has caused a seismic tremor in the socio-political establishment. Most remarkably, it has done so on the engine of a non-monetary economy.

These alternative economies, for lack of a better word, have emerged in myriad applications and disciplines – as enabled by the connective tissue of the Internet – and crowdsourcing has proven to be wildly successful as a means of developing them. Crowdsourcing, in a general sense, is the practice of soliciting content – whether ideas, actions or labor – from the public at large, in order to achieve a particular goal. Wikipedia(.com), for example, has become a multilingual, crowdsourced digital juggernaut of information since its launch in 2001. It is within the conceptual lineage of the *Encyclopædia Britannica*, the original leather-bound repository of all knowledge (and perhaps, even, a descendent of Tomas Aquinas' *Summa Theologica*, begun in 1265 and growing until St Thomas' death in 1274). From its beginnings in 1768, *Britannica* was the first such document to operate under "continuous revision" (a process of constant reprinting that was officially institutionalized only in 1933). But it is a closed system: *Britannica*'s board of editors is a discreet cadre populated by the intellectual elite, and its regenerative process has, to date, operated on a scale of decades. On the other hand, Wikipedia – the young gun, *Britannica*'s unruly child – responds with a lightning-quick system of peer editing and review, in which content is generated and vetted instantaneously by volunteers (that is, anyone willing to click "edit"). The running joke is that Wikipedia only works in practice...in theory, it is impossible. There is no compensation, and users freely offer their intellectual contributions, both content and editing – once again, an economy of reputation and altruism.

In its wake, the foundational cultural institution of *Britannica* couldn't help but capitulate to a rising digital tide; in 2012 – eleven years after the birth of Wikipedia – *Britannica* made the announcement that it would discontinue printing and segue to an exclusively online presence.[19] Whether or not crowdsourced information makes rational or economic sense, the bottom line is that collective wisdom is being poured into the Internet at an incredible rate, and it is changing the structure of human knowledge.

In these cases, the substrate of the sharing ecology is digital. However, the results of online crowdsourcing are not strictly confined to bits and bytes; digital networks are becoming a forum for physical objects and services through tools such as Airbnb, RelayRides, Lyft, and SnapGoods. The first rumbling, of course, was eBay's network of citizen retail, but today connective applications are becoming increasingly specialized and easier to use. And, inevitably, there is a simultaneous shift from sharing for free to sharing for a fee.

The greatest success story is Brian Chesky's Airbnb – a project that started with a couple of air mattresses for rent during a San Francisco design conference and skyrocketed into a multi-million-dollar company. The website allows anyone with a spare room to snap a photograph, set a price, list it online, and be connected with visitors in need of a bed – essentially to operate a personal hotel. Today, there are hundreds of thousands of listings in countries across the globe. And it isn't just rooms. "We have over six hundred castles. We have dozens of yurts, caves, tepees with TVs in them, water towers, motor homes, private islands, glass houses, lighthouses, igloos with Wi-Fi; we have a home that Jim Morrison used to live in; we have treehouses – hundreds of treehouses...."[20] There was a period of time in 2011 when users could log on and rent the entirety of Liechtenstein, listed by Prince Hans-Adam II, for seventy thousand dollars a night. The Internet has evolved from a tool for communication to a collective encyclopedia...and now a platform for everyone to participate in building the world's largest citizen-hotel.

As yet, the most thriving sectors have been cars and housing, but collective consumption is spreading. There are constellations of services emerging around Airbnb and in parallel to it (house cleaning, taxis, personalized tours, car rental) seemingly across every facet of society. A 2013 *Economist* magazine article on the subject ran a humorous illustration labeled "Room, $38/night; Pickup truck, $9/hour; Hermès Birkin Bag, $100/party."[21] As the momentum builds, various projects have attempted to serve as consolidators of "collective consumerism," as it has come to be called, because the success of an alternative economy ultimately hinges on a critical mass of participants. The metrics are simple: once enough physical "stuff" is available online, it will become the most practical solution, because of proximity and variety, and its membership will expand virally. One such platform is Google Mine – a system integrated with Google+ that will allow users to catalog, share, and track every single possession. "Google Mine lets you organize the things you own, use, wish for, and more: gadgets, clothing, electronics, DVDs, cars, bikes or anything!"[22] Most importantly, it is a feature of Google's social media network based on relationships between friends, relatives, and co-workers.

That, precisely, is the crux of the sharing economy: it is social. It is less about quantifiable, financial, extrinsic gains and more about social gains on the order of reputation, so-called "sustainable lifestyle," and community-ties. From an individual standpoint, sharing is financially logical: network connectivity is increasing exponentially, while material resources are being depleted. It makes sense to save both. But the crucial point is, above all, social desirability. Human action depends upon rewards, both financial and interpersonal, and collective consumerism emerges as a response to both, just as Linux was driven by a heady mix of altruism and aggrandizement. It is as if the theory of "conspicuous consumption"[23] outlined by economist Thorstein Veblen (1857–1929) were turned upside down – becoming a no-less-socially driven "conspicuous collectivity." The standing of an individual within a collective is a powerful non-monetary reward, providing the necessary incentive for alternative economies. A 2003 scientific paper found that "social and environmental concern and action, it turns out, are based on more than simply access to the facts (a finding that may seem obvious, but has often proven difficult to fully acknowledge). In reality, both seem to be motivated above all by a particular set of underlying values."[24] And not just values, but also defaults and norms, as noted by political philosopher and Harvard Professor Michael Sandel in his work on the moral limits of markets.[25] Modernity assumed that Industrial production and services can only take place within market norms; one disruption of the Web is not just the empowerment of the "long tail" (the many small players) it is also – for the first time in modern history – that we are building production tools and services driven by social and cultural norms in addition to market forces. Put simply, amateurism is going to scale.[26] Vibrant ties within an active community are crucial: they constitute its substance and its action and they distill its norms. Sociability is the same ineffable force recurring throughout creative history, an intuitive system that reflects our ingrained need for interrelatedness.

Just as it did for open-source software production and the consumer economy, the Internet is shattering the boundaries of civic action. In addition to crowdsourced software-coding and crowdsourced ownership, the Internet has made it possible to crowdsource...a crowd.

The means of public action was thrown open by the events of the 2010 Arab Spring – a series of revolutions in the Arab world ignited by social media. The ubiquitous and instantaneous connectivity of tools including Facebook and Twitter allowed ideas to spread like wildfire through a population, and for consequent protests to be organized in real time. A March 2011 survey revealed that during the course of the events, an overwhelming majority (88% in Egypt and 94% in Tunisia) used social media sites as their primary information outlet.[27] Revolution itself was the overlay of digital networks onto the space of architecture and public action, and there it achieved gravity. Just as the *cocarde tricolore* was a potent spark in the French revolution (the small red white and blue ribbon that revolutionaries pinned to their chest) so too was #Egypt a symbol and a tool: it had 1.4 million hits in just three months (#Jan25 had 1.2 million and #protest had 620,000), and it spilled directly into the physical space of the city.[28]

Collective action has the tremendous power to burn holes straight through existing social and economic fabrics, but can the same networks – the same networked mentality – be used constructively? August 2011 saw riots across the United Kingdom, sparked by altercations between citizens and law enforcement. Tension accelerated as dissidents quickly organized gatherings using mobile devices and social media, and the events soon came to be known as "The BlackBerry riots." Yet, in the wake of these riots, the same technological tools were applied in an entirely different way. The movement began with a single tweet by @sophontrack that suggested citizens respond positively to the chaos around them. Demonstrating the power of a simple idea, a wave of re-tweets crystallized as riotcleanup.co.uk – a website launched within minutes to establish times and locations for the cleanup operation. Soon thousands of people had aggregated into cleaning groups, and almost instantaneously, users of Twitter linked through #riotcleanup had gathered in the same streets that were torn apart by violence. The momentum carried to cities outside of London and ultimately more than ninety thousand people were involved cleaning the streets.[29] "#riotcleanup started not as an organization – but an idea, an idea to change what was a downfall in society into something positive."[30]

On the other side of the world, just months after political and social tensions erupted in 2013, the fiery conflict in Turkey's Taksim Gezi Park left a vacuum of social agendas in its wake, but it also created a tightly knit communal spirit. "Gezi helped awaken in many of us a sense of sharing and solidarity. It might be the best thing coming out of the protests and the following period,"[31] said resident Aysu Erdo du in an interview. Citizens acted on and nurtured the connections that had seared the city of Istanbul during protests, and initiatives built from the bottom up have gained a strong foothold – as hackathons, markets, creative groups and forums. The mutual reinforcement of digital and physical connectivity has created a robust – and productive – citizen network.

• • • • • • • •

In the 20th and 21st centuries, new tools of connectivity based on the Internet have dramatically expanded the dynamics of human action and interaction. And those human connections refuse to linger sequestered in the Cloud. Whether it is online sci-fi communities organizing a convention, enterprising individuals offering their spare bedrooms as hotel rooms, or engaged citizens fighting for their lives and liberties, physical space has proven to be a vital counterpart of digital existence.

Bits and atoms are inseparably linked by human sociability. Today it is nearly impossible to remain unaffected by the Internet, and ordinary people are vigorously and innovatively bringing it into their physical world with face-to-face tools for the networked era. The coder sitting next door in his pajamas is writing the urban apps that may be implemented from India to Panama. Rallying cries of a new government begin as 140-character chunks. It is a paradigm shift on the order of the global village, but one that is connective and discursive.

This can only be described as a sea-change in the scope of human interaction, sociability and global connectivity, one that has engulfed almost every facet of culture – save architecture. Why can't open sourcing, a methodology that commands almost limitless potential in the digital world (proven time and again by the likes of Mozilla, Airbnb, and the Internet itself), and which has existed throughout the history of architecture, have the same transformative effect on contemporary design and building practice? Where is the Linux of homes or offices or libraries? Page through any design magazine – you won't find a building without a signature. The world of architecture circles on its well-worn orbit, seemingly outside the gravitational pull of networked participation.

Can architecture really remain aloof? The same energetic participation that drives Etsy, fantasy football and Tahrir Square could pump a collective vigor into architecture. The success of software is a direct provocation for architecture's paradigm shift, orders of magnitude beyond that of the stone arch or steel-and-glass construction. How can the new tools available to the architect bring people together – not only to inhabit, but to change, augment, and ultimately create the environment around them?

5
·········

Open Source Gets Physical: How Digital Collaboration Technologies Became Tangible

Instead of talking about it,
I'd give people the tools. This
wasn't meant to be provocative
or important, but we put together
these fab labs…and they exploded
around the world.

Neil Gershenfeld, *"Unleash Your Creativity in a Fab Lab"*, 2006[1]

On a blustery New England day in 2001, a knot of MIT researchers scurried across campus, down the staircase of building E14,
and into a basement lab that thrummed with the energy of warm
machines and white-hot ideas. They were part of a group of MIT
students, professors, and researchers – including some of the
adjunct editors and authors of this book – who for years spent
their nights in a space with no official title but "the basement."
The underground space was a haphazardly assembled fabrication lab with a single goal: to create. Here, a hacker mentality
launched ideas into physical space, with an assortment of laser
cutters, vacuum formers, 3D printers and hypersonic waterjet
cutters. It was a well-kept secret, the kind of equipment treasure
trove that DIYers inhabit when they dream. Quite literally – the
basement lab was in use at all hours of the day and night, and the
people keeping an around-the-clock vigil became a close community of fabrication-minded innovators.

   Close...and closed. As he observed from his office next
door, Professor Neil Gershenfeld was concerned that this had
become a secluded cult of fabrication. He was bothered by the
limited accessibility of such a remarkable creative resource. An
opportunity like this one – the almost limitless potential of using
fabrication technology to jump out of binary and into physical
space – should be open and free. Tools should be in the hands of
whoever would use them, and Gershenfeld suspected that such
willingness might emerge on MIT campus. He was gripped by
the notion of construction as education: "'Constructionism' is
grounded in the idea that people learn by actively constructing

new knowledge rather than by having information 'poured' into their heads...people learn with particular effectiveness when they are engaged in constructing personally meaningful artifacts (such as computer programs, animations, or robots)."[2] Gershenfeld imagined that the basement lab, or something like it, would be the crux of a fabrication-empowered learning model.

Determined, now, to realize an idea that was beginning to take shape, the group of students, faculty and researchers who had coalesced in "the basement" began collecting as many resources as possible – tools and machinery scattered about the MIT campus – and simultaneously orchestrated a collaboration between the Grassroots Invention Group (GIG) and the newly minted Center for Bits and Atoms. Within a matter of months (not to mention kickstart funding from the National Science Foundation, NSF), fabrication at MIT had gone from – literally – an underground operation, to become one of the most exciting programs at MIT: a digital fabrication laboratory, known as the "Fab Lab."

In broad strokes, the Fab Lab explored the relationship between digital information and its physical manifestation. The overarching goal was to explore the potential of education-through-building and of bringing together bottom-up communities through technology. This was an unprecedented direction for learning (within a traditional academic setting such as MIT), and an entirely new resource for people who would never have considered themselves "designers."

A certain chemistry happened, between the buffet of equipment, new modes of learning, personal empowerment, and possibilities for tangible expressions of digital work. Student interest erupted. When Gershenfeld announced a new class called How to Make Almost Anything, hundreds of people showed up for the first day. This simple idea of learning by making and crossing the digital/physical divide was generating a staggering amount of enthusiasm. In response to this overwhelmingly full booking of eager students, Gershenfeld began to turn his attention outward. Considering that the opportunity for fabrication had provoked this much excitement on campus, what kind of response would fab labs find in the world at large?

In conjunction with the NSF, Gershenfeld began setting up similar spaces outside of MIT, and sparked a meteoric propagation of fab labs worldwide. "Instead of talking about it, I'd give people the tools. This wasn't meant to be provocative or important, but we put together these 'Fab Labs.' And they exploded around the globe."[3] Fab labs cropped up everywhere, from campuses to inner cities to rural villages, and the projects coming out of them were locally inflected in an entirely new way (at a Fab Lab in Norway, for example, shepherds put together radio-frequency ID tags for tracking wandering sheep).[4] "There is really a fabrication and instrumentation divide bigger than the digital divide…. We're just at the edge of this digital revolution in fabrication, where the output of computation programs the physical world."[5] This was a new form empowerment – fab labs allowed people to modify or "hack" the world around them, rather than passively absorbing information or products. As a result, ideas began gushing out of the quickly multiplying fab lab network. As people designed and constructed technology themselves, it became localized, instrumental, and practical. Even more importantly, as they were established, labs started hosting weekly classes, workshops and social events, becoming nuclei of design communities.

Propelled by the physical and social space of fab labs, a powerful idea – one based on a different understanding of education, experimentation, and making – emerged from the dank MIT basement to become a worldwide network of citizen-empowerment. In 2006 Gershenfeld stood in front of a global audience at TED and stated: "The message coming from the fab labs is that the other five billion people on the planet [the poorest ninety-nine percent] aren't just technical sinks, they're sources." He said, "The real opportunity is to harness the inventive power of the world, to locally design and produce solutions to local problems."[6]

••••••••

The energy that created the Internet is a seemingly infinite web of connections and nodes, and what made it possible was a new definition of ownership. Its fate was sealed during the 1990s when a collective decision was made to maintain the Internet as a "free and open" system. The structure of the Internet is essentially a network of dumb pipes that carries a messy system of information packets (known as TCP/IP routing), rather than a clean, efficient – but costly – manicured system that might have been established and maintained by the telcos of the world. Open and wild versus costly and clean. To make an analogy with software, the same activity takes the form of shared source code versus corporate software development. Linus Torvalds showed that putting the "kernel" of a new operating system (Linux) into the hands of coders-at-large can elicit a groundswell of participation across the globe.

But what does all of this look like in physical space? It is one thing to send lines of code across digital networks, but an entirely different matter to share...well, matter.

Open-source architecture is more than soliciting feed-back, and a thriving collaboration is more than inviting many people to join the design process (it is certainly not, as today's most common justification suggests, starting an architecture project as a design competition[7]). During the 1960s, it became obvious that so-called "participatory design" is an almost one-way street of endless questionnaires and begrudging stake-holder responses, whereas the magnetic energy of people coming together is a viral, powerful, unconstrained force that accretes as it accelerates, beyond the limits of top-down initiatives. As users join behind a common purpose, collaboration reaches a critical mass of input and output. It is a chemical reaction that happens when a "recursive public"[8] (a term coined by cultural theorist Christopher Kelty to describe a group of people who are concerned with the propagation of that which makes them a group of people) is given the reigns.

The primordial example is cooking: a basic unit of sociability, guided by communal activity over the length of human history. Culinary traditions reflect and shape social interactions in any given community, and are also changed, added to, transformed, and passed on as the beginnings of an open-source cultural genealogy. Information is shared, rather than matter, and as such it can be easily distributed and modified, taking on a history of its own.

Digital production was dramatically transformed by a new means of effectively sharing ideas, and the same thing is now becoming possible – even advantageous – in physical space. British economist John Maynard Keynes (1883–1946) shrewdly observed that it is easier to ship recipes than cakes and biscuits. The simple statement is compelling, almost blindingly obvious – and yet it is not how the world's industrial economy works. Alastair Parvin contends that we are moving into a world where the recipes will become the most valuable thing on earth, and yet simultaneously they should be free. "Expect legal battles."[9]

Design can, in theory, be shared and distributed in the same way as recipes communicate food. In 1974, Enzo Mari – considered "one of the most thoughtful and intellectually provocative designers of the late 20th century,"[10] – presented exactly that: a furniture collection that does not fit categorically into the world of atoms. It took shape as a line of wooden pieces called *"Autoprogettazione"* (self-design), a set of chairs, tables, bookshelves, beds, etc. – presented and sold as a list of do-it-yourself instructions. These documents allow anyone to build, modify, and adapt a cohesive set of furniture in their home or garage, all without power tools (yet today, somewhat ironically, a luxurious kit of beautiful pre-cut wood pieces by Mari is available from Finnish furniture house Artek[11]).

Autoprogettazione, like Linux, is still driven by the basic idea of sharing code. The instructions for assembling the furniture are a kind of information – an intangible genetic material for design – to be communicated and distributed. Aside from "hack" esthetics and a rhetoric of personal agency, there are deeper questions raised by such a project: Who, really, is the author of the "Enzo Mari chair" I just built with my own two hands? What if I sell it? What if another company starts producing a kit like Artek's? Could they be sued? These all point toward a somewhat archaic notion of authorship, ownership and copyright. The latter is defined as the specific legal structure that allows a national government to grant exclusive rights of ownership to the creator of a work – that is, specifically, the right to copy, produce derivatives, perform or display, and, most importantly, to benefit financially from it. Under this umbrella, computer code is now acknowledged and appropriated. Copyright began as a response to the printing press, and it is now standard authorial protection for almost everything, from literature, music, images, and intellectual property to art, architecture, and consumer products.

In his reactionary 1983 *GNU Manifesto* (GNU is the operating system named as a recursive acronym for *GNU's Not Unix!*), programmer and activist Richard Stallman proposed an idea he called "copyleft": a system in which copyright law would be massaged such that any given work could be free and open for modification. Furthermore, every subsequent iteration – whether modified, augmented or elaborated – would be free as well. In the manifesto, reprinted for the broader public in programmers' magazine *Dr. Dobb's Journal* in 1985, Stallman wrote that "GNU is not in the public domain. Everyone will be permitted to modify and redistribute GNU, but no distributor will be allowed to restrict its further redistribution. That is to say, proprietary modifications will not be allowed. I want to make sure that all versions of GNU remain free."[12] The system was predicated on an entirely new conception of rights and ownership: authorship evolved.

Two decades later, at the turn of the millennium, the same question of proprietary authorship continued to plague Harvard academic and activist Lawrence Lessig. He found copyleft to be just as strict – albeit the polar opposite – as copyright, and sought to articulate a flexible middle ground. Through his scholarly and civic work on rights, he conceived of a more systematic form of open protection, what he called a "creative commons." Lessig's non-profit organization, founded in 2001, published a series of licenses that are free for public use; documents that enable creators to choose which rights they reserve as their own and which they waive for the benefit of the public. "The author" (whatever that now means) is no longer the sole, hermetic, inviolable proprietor of his work, but rather the originary branch of a tree that sprouts twigs and buds with each additional collaborator. Rather than the black and white schism between copyright and copyleft, a Creative Commons license becomes a tailor-made set of rights. This legal structure facilitates a delicate balance between controlled creative development and chaotic participation.

As such systems have propagated and enabled an increasing number of projects, they have proven that the benefits of moderated sharing go beyond altruistic or esthetic ends. A Creative Commons license gives the possibility of an astronomical degree of public visibility – while still crediting the intellectual and esthetic contributions of the author and subsequent modifiers – and has completely changed both amateur and professional creativity. In her work *The Future of Creative Commons,* Cathy Casserly, Creative Commons' CEO, wrote, "People used to think of reuse as stealing; today, not letting others use your work can mean irrelevance."[13]

Estimates point toward over five hundred million works currently licensed through Creative Commons, particularly weighted toward such media platforms as YouTube, Wikimedia Commons and Flickr. In its mitigation of the constraints of copyright law (particularly for the average person making a YouTube video), a Creative Commons license is the tool that enables a creator to take advantage of the full collaborative potential of the network around him. Creative Commons allows anyone to reuse, augment and adapt anything from a logo to a piece of furniture, while still citing the original designer. Flexibility, evolution, and adaptation are possible, but the powerful impetus of human motivation remains intact: acknowledgement of authorship. The chair in your living room might have been nailed together by your own hand – even modified – but still bears the signature of the original creator, Enzo Mari, *Autoprogettazione,* 1974.

Creative Commons is a fulfillment of the whimsical social-design theory that Mari had posited decades earlier – or rather, it is a legalistic tool for implementing Mari's ideas for shared production and design. Now that such a statutory measure of protection is in place, the other side of the coin is physical and spatial: an open-ended platform, or freeing agent, for the substantive production of shared ideas. It is only logical that the first and most successful instance of physical open sourcing should have happened at the intersection of the digital and material worlds. It is cheap, adaptable and ubiquitous, but, most importantly, it makes sharing and building physical ideas as easy as sharing and executing lines of code: the Arduino.

An Arduino is a tiny piece of hardware, a single board adorned with various circuits surrounding an 8 or 32-bit microcontroller. Its digital shadow is a simple software, called the Integrated Development Environment, that enables users to write lines of code to control the Arduino's various functions. Code is shared openly via Creative Commons, and can be used and adapted by anyone. The system is essentially a bridge between digital and physical, turning script into action. Internet theorist Clay Shirky posted in an online forum, "An increasing number of physical products are becoming so data-centric that the physical aspects are simply executional steps at the end of a chain of digital manipulation."[14] That is, there is a shrinking distinction between the physical and the digital world, and Creative Commons is the enabler of fluid sharing within and across them.

The tiny, open-ended microprocessor is igniting a sea-change in production and design mentality, a shift toward so-called "physical computing." Arduinos have become the base unit of personal fabrication (or "hacking," to use the popular terminology), allowing any gadget to sense its environment, get online, control other electronic devices, or communicate with one another. You might attach an Arduino to a thermometer and program it to send you a text message when it's cold out… and someone else might turn that around and make an Arduino-controlled crock pot. These kinds of "hack" objects are smart, but most importantly, ideas are shared. Everything from detailed plans for building your own Arduino to lines of code for animating it to do almost anything are free and open for use and adaptation.

This is a tectonic shift in collaborative production mentality, and it is not confined to the Arduino platform. The same kinds of projects are cropping up around the world and across disciplines – other microcontrollers like Raspberry Pi all the way to LEGO Mindstorms (a collaboration with the MIT Media Lab). These are a more technological manifestation of the same energy that has always driven humans to cook together, share food, and develop culinary traditions. Sharing and collaborating are simple human impulses, and now – using the connective platform of the Internet and production tools such as fab labs and Arduinos – they can. As Keynes noted, there is more value in the recipe than the cake.

What was formerly a linear (dead-end) distribution from creator to consumer has now become an accelerated feedback loop with plural creative input – and a plethora of projects and platforms are emerging to bridge the gap between digital and physical. A project called OScar began as a manifesto and an online forum, with the goal of designing a cheap, easy-to-produce car by an entirely decentralized design process.[15] The project was soon followed by OSGV (Open-Source Green Vehicle), which sought to implement an open-design process to address problems of sustainable mobility. Designed by a core team of developers and a constellation of contributors, a seven-passenger SUV was collaboratively engineered and produced by a start-up company.[16] Far outside the automotive world, a project called Free Beer (or Vores Øl, in the founders' native Danish) translates the principles of Free Software into tens of thousands of liters of brew: anyone can download its recipe, tweak it, and sell their own distinctive beer. Today the Free Beer mark is produced by two full-scale breweries in Copenhagen and Zurich and micro-breweries around the world.[17] The Neuros Open-Source Device is a non-proprietary media center (based on Linux, of course!) that can record and store content from virtually any source in a standard format.[18] And there is the much-publicized (mildly unsettling, but primarily witty) RepRap – a 3D printer that can only be constructed with parts printed by another RepRap.[19]

There is no single trajectory for an open-source project, nor is the outcome really ever anticipated. A post on the online RepRap forum states that "Open project evolution is somewhat Darwinian. Many fall by the wayside and are abandoned, some fork into newer and better projects leaving the parent behind, some just keep on going successfully."[20] The single commonality between all of them is that the entire process is driven by a collective energy – the motive force of open-source evolution, to continue the metaphor. Paola Antonelli, Architecture and Design curator at MoMA, New York, termed it a "new hacker culture,"[21] sparked by a perfect storm of interrelated projects including *MAKE:* magazine (and its Maker Faires), Processing (the universal programming language), the Arduino (what Antonelli called "the magical board that sits at the very foundation of the contemporary physical open-source universe"),[22] and the Makerbot (a low-cost 3D printer).

"It is, of course, brought to life by the act of tinkering productively, experimenting, testing, re-testing and adjusting, and all the while enjoying it with many like-minded spirits and engaging with the world in an open, constructive collaboration with colleagues and other specialists. In other words, in open-source mode,"[23] Antonelli concluded.

This shift in the process of design and fabrication is even causing tremors in traditional production industries. Companies have become aware of the creative and constructive potential at their fingertips, and are struggling to implement a hybridized top-down and bottom-up model. They have identified the incredible energy of hackers and tinkerers around the globe as a renewable resource, ripe for harvesting (or, to cast it in a more cynical light: why should companies finance an R&D department when they can crowdsource for free, with the same net technological result?). Some companies are embracing an ethos of "release early, release often" – usually buggy, unfinished, beta versions of products – but even those half-baked projects are eagerly grabbed and modified by early adopters. Product development becomes a collaboration between consumers and corporations in a process of mutual tinkering, feedback and fabrication.

It seems like the last discipline to stir is architecture. The Arduino actively grants a voice to anyone interested in speaking through technology, and people around the world are coming together to co-create in an ever-expanding open-source hacker ecosystem. The idea of collapsing the traditional distinction between designer and user seems to have its ultimate fulfillment in open-source architecture. Why not hack your house? Where is the open-source mall? How can you tinker with office buildings or supermarkets? These spaces shape our everyday lives...how would that change if we took an active role in shaping them?

In 1964 Cedric Price stated: "I consider it unlikely that architecture and planning will match the contribution Hush Puppies have made to society today, let alone approach that of the transistor or loop, until a total reappraisal of its particular expertise is self-imposed, or inflicted from outside. Designers and architects would be better employed in devising new languages of comparison from computers, than in using them to confirm the obvious."[24]

Cedric Price's inflammatory statement echoes today as an increasingly urgent call-to-arms for architects and designers, as the cybernetics he only imagined become an implementable reality. The "total reappraisal of [architecture's] particular expertise" could be an open-source mentality, and the "new languages" could look a lot like Creative Commons. Now that these systems exist, voices are beginning to echo from the peripheries of architecture to answer Price.

In 2006, Cameron Sinclair proposed an Open Architecture Network (openarchitecturenetwork.org) – an online, open-source platform to which designers can contribute, implementing change in the built environment, specifically for the developing world. In his speech for the acceptance of the 2006 TED Prize, Sinclair described his experience of founding the organization: "What it showed me is that there's a grassroots movement going on of socially responsible designers who really believe that this world has got a lot smaller, and that we have the opportunity – not the responsibility, but the opportunity – to really get involved in making change."[25] Most importantly, Sinclair describes it as "a grassroots movement": the project is driven by his discovery (or provocation) of an energetic community of "socially responsible designers" and he is seeking a means of mobilizing that public. Specifically, the constituents of the movement will be empowered by a universal platform that allows anyone to contribute – whether they are architects or citizens – and it will organize those contributions in the most effective way possible. Sinclair's TED Wish, the OAN, incorporates and enables users to:

- Share ideas, designs, and plans;
- View and review designs posted by others;
- Collaborate with each other, people in other professions, and community leaders, to address specific design challenges;
- Manage design projects from concept to implementation;
- Communicate easily among team members;
- Protect their intellectual property rights using the Creative Commons "some rights reserved" licensing system and be shielded from unwarranted liability;
- Build a more sustainable future.[26]

The responsibilities of architectural construction, design, maintenance, and so on, are invested in many different stakeholders, but seamlessly integrated into one system. The Open Architecture Network includes a measure of intellectual property protection, incentivizing users – specifically, trained architects and designers – to participate in a rigorous way. Yet, because the platform has embedded design and view/review functionality, the end user is also empowered to design, or at least to guide design decisions.

"Far from replacing the traditional architect, the goal of the [Open Architecture Network] is to allow designers to work together in a whole new way, a way that enables five billion potential clients [the poorest ninety-nine percent] to access their skills and expertise. The network has a simple mission: to generate not one idea but the hundreds of thousands of design ideas needed to improve living conditions for all."[27] The Open Architecture Network becomes a free marketplace for design, with a very real allure for both user groups: for trained architects, of having a design physically constructed and improving living conditions, and for those in need, of receiving an effective and locally optimized building (or rather, an architectural intervention of some type).

Although the Open Architecture Network is still being realized, Sinclair's "Wish" (in broad strokes) has already come true. WikiHouse[28] is an online, open-source platform of user-generated housing designs that anyone can download, "print" with plywood on a CNC mill, and snap together like IKEA furniture or a life-size puzzle (it even comes with a convenient plywood hammer). In the words of its co-founder Alastair Parvin: "Ultimately, WikiHouse is not about a single construction type, but an open, accessible, adaptable system. It almost becomes a sort of coding language for physical space."[29] The plans for each WikiHouse are generated with SketchUp – a free, intuitive 3D modeling software – and are available through Creative Commons at no cost.

The first prototype house went up in under twenty-four hours, including cutting and assembly, all with a staggeringly low price tag (as houses go). But the specifics of cost and time are somewhat irrelevant, at this point (like any technology, it will continue to get cheaper and quicker): the importance is how a system like this empowers design. As designer Nick Lerodiaconou (of oo:/, the London design studio behind WikiHouse) comments,

"The driving question beneath something like WikiHouse is whether technology can meaningfully lower the threshold for design and fabrication, and thus democratize making in the same way that the home printer democratized the printing press, or YouTube democratized broadcasting."[30]

Despite Parvin's efforts and the ground that WikiHouse has covered, quick building printers still have a distance to come before the idea is universally implemented. In the interim, each link in the design and production chain can nonetheless be infused with open sourcing – from funding to production to assembly.

The collective momentum, then, is not restricted to design. Although funding is traditionally the purview of philanthropists or wealthy corporations, it has now become democratized by crowd-funding platforms such as Kickstarter.[31] With a modicum of video-making knowledge (which, thanks to YouTube and Creative Commons, is nearly universal) anyone can launch a passionate message to the Internet-at-large and wait for funds to echo back. Through Sitra,[32] a Finnish innovation fund, Dan Hill proposed a rough and ready physical version of Kickstarter called Brickstarter.[33] The platform is aimed more toward community participation and Internet-enabled neo-barn-raising. That is, responses to a Brickstarter campaign would less likely be cash than an eager, boot-shod twenty-something with a shovel. Goteo[34] is a platform developed and launched in Spain that effectively collapses Kickstarter and Brickstarter, enabling distributed collaboration by allowing designers to solicit specific kinds of contribution – from services, to funding to microtasks and anything in between.[35] Estate Guru[36] is a somewhat more mature platform with similar aims – aggregating funds to facilitate architectural production. The sum total is that real, tangible projects – which would never before have gained enough traction – could take off thanks to Internet-megaphone platforms. A functional Brickstarter platform was never launched, and many other initiatives of its ilk will suffer the high mortality rate of startups. The importance is not in the name or the specific platform, but the broader momentum towards collective funding as well as design.

Paola Antonelli was right: every ingredient of a "new hacker culture" is here. Networks for sharing information and ideas (the Internet and its communities); protection for authors and a system of easily managing rights (Creative Commons); tools for implementing design in physical space (Arduinos, 3D printers, CNC mills); and the means – financial or manpower – to make it happen (Kickstarter and its family). These constitute the engine that will drive the accelerating force of collective production.

You are a designer. Making is democratized.

• • • • • • • •

Productive, collaborative, shared design is happening around the world, and it is only accelerating. Yet as it becomes increasingly mainstream for software and consumer goods, the open-source mentality has been muscled out of architecture by traditional practice and remains in the murky periphery, away from the discipline's spotlight. A reductive categorization is that architecture still operates under the authorship model of copyright, when design, media, and culture are moving toward copyleft and Creative Commons. Almost all disciplines are rapidly expanding in scope while architecture progresses tentatively.

It would be difficult to find a major technology or science magazine that has not yet run a cover story on DIY, fabrication or the "Arduino revolution," but participatory architecture is far from the covers of *Architectural Digest*, *Dwell*, *Abitare*, or *Wallpaper**. It is marginalized by a world still clinging to the names and signatures of its genius creators. Media outlets find it hard to talk about a project in terms of not one, but many authors. When was the last time you saw a *Dezeen* post on the generic?[37]

Media loves the cult of the celebrity architect. In 2011, *Abitare* ran a full issue titled "Being Jean Nouvel," with the tagline: "Jean Nouvel unveils to *Abitare* his private and public life. Who is he? Which are his friends? How does he use his time? What does he do? With whom does he work?"[38]...only the most recent in a series of profiles that includes Norman Foster, Renzo Piano and Zaha Hadid. In Japan, Tadao Ando's media-beguiling pedigree as a truck-driver-turned-boxer-turned-architect is typified by the popular anecdote in which the enraged perfectionistic architect strikes down a construction worker with a one-hit knockout. The same idea has inspired filmmakers as well; a 2011 *FastCo Design* article[39] reviewed a documentary about the Eameses, praising the filmmaker's "willingness to probe the Eameses' (especially Charles's) less-than-saintly habits, giv[ing] the film an unexpected edge." Not to be outdone, *Architectural Record* ran a review of *The Competition* (2013), titled "Starchitects Face Off in New Film;"[40] the same film was elsewhere enthusiastically hailed as a "documentary where architects stop being polite and start getting real"[41] – it all sounds uncannily like reality television. This is what it looks like when the 21st-century media machine lionizes the Promethean architect.

The media is fixing its camera in the wrong direction. It is focused on the individual, but missing the broader implications of a shift in the discipline. Comparing the sheer productivity and number of people designing (not to be confused with "designers") might tell a different story than those printed in magazines. Not only that – a more important question is: does open sourcing even need mainstream media? How relevant is a cover story when WikiHouse is poised "to make it possible for almost anyone, regardless of their formal skills, to freely download and build structures which are affordable and suited to their needs?"[42]

"The factor[ies] of the future may look more like weavers' cottages than Ford's assembly line,"[43]...an uncharacteristically bold statement from the pages of *The Economist*. The implication is that democratization of production will revisit the "timeless way of building," the forms of production that yielded anonymous or vernacular architecture. Most notably, this will have a dramatic impact on urban economies and the production of the built environment. Parvin speculates that in the future we may look back on the monolithic, top-down, financially-capitalized, one-size-fits-all models of architectural production as an awkward, adolescent blip in mankind's industrial development.[44] The idea of bottom-up, locally-adapted, copied typologies, produced by citizens using their social capital as well as their financial capital, is far from new. In many ways it is bringing technology to pre-industrial "barn-raising" approaches.

Open-source architecture is presented as an innovation, but it is really just the vernacular with an Internet connection. Local design fueled by a global community.

The challenge is looming, goals are clear and technologies for achieving them exist. The task, then, is to reflect on the potential implications that "future vernacular" will have on economic development, social justice, resource scarcity, labor economies, planning systems, and the role of professionals. The discipline cannot remain hermetically sealed forever – there is a critical mass of people, ready and willing to work in a bottom-up way. A tipping point is approaching that posits architecture as information and brings empowerment through fabrication. The boundaries of the discipline will be exploded outward by sharing marketplaces, building-scale "Thingiverses," "remixes" of iconic buildings, fab labs for homes, open-source plans and 3D models, or the architectural Arduino. And when it does, will you hack your house?

6

·········

Building Harmonies:
Toward a Choral Architect

In reality, architecture has
become too important to be
left to architects.

Giancarlo de Carlo, *Architecture's Public*, 1970[1]

During the summer of 2006, Annie Choi – a recent graduate of Columbia's School of Arts writing program – hunched over her laptop, typing quickly despite the noise of the New York City streets outside and the heat trapped in her apartment. Perhaps because she was relegated to a cramped 187-square-foot studio without air conditioning and "four pieces of furniture, total,"[2] she harbored festering resentment. On her screen was an open letter to architects, its first words: "Dear Architects, I am sick of your shit."[3]

Through her network of architect friends, Choi had come to know the editors of *Pidgin Magazine* – a recently founded annual publication based at the Princeton School of Architecture. The first issue of the magazine had been quite rigorous: a self-proclaimed "dispatch" from within the school to communicate architectural work and ideas to the outside world, taking shape as 256 (very well-designed) pages of theory, renderings, project descriptions (what amounted to "abstract blah-blah," according to Choi). Very high-level, of course, so the editors reasoned that the second issue might need a breath of fresh air. It would be great to invite a non-architect to contribute, and better yet, why not their friend – an up-and-coming young writer based in New York?

Choi was about to publish her first book, *Happy Birthday or Whatever*,[4] finding her wry, irreverent voice through "humorous essays about family and, as I like to call it, 'stupid shit I love to talk about.'"[5] Her work had nothing to do with architecture, but sketched emotional, unpolished accounts of personal experience. The open letter on her screen emerged from what she called her "complicated relationship to architecture, which is to say that I don't really give two poops to the wind about it, but all my friends are architects and the only thing architects talk about is architecture."[6]

Whether or not the editors expected it, Choi delivered a scathing deadpan criticism. The open letter unapologetically made fun of the culture of architecture…"but you know, in a loving way."[7]

After dense pages of *Pidgin*'s cutting-edge academic discourse on architecture, the letter from Choi was a jab in the ribs. She casually announced to the architecture community that they were irrelevant: architects "all design glass dildos that I will never work or live in and serve only to obstruct my view of New Jersey…I do not care about architecture. It is true. This is what I do care about: burritos; hedgehog; coffee. As you can see, architecture is not on the list. I believe that architecture falls somewhere between toenail fungus and invasive colonoscopy in the list of things that interest me."[8] Behind the indelicate language, Choi was actually making an incisive criticism: architects, look around you. Don't take yourselves so seriously, and spend a moment to think about the people you are designing for.

Responses to the letter were violent. Choi had hit a nerve. Hate mail poured in from architects around the world, demanding respect or challenging her to enroll in a graduate program on architectural theory before proffering an opinion. But by the same token, the letter gained considerable momentum and support. Architects who felt trapped in the system and culture of architecture identified with its refreshing perspective. The letter put into words – in the frank, readable language that architects cannot seem to get onto a page – the extent to which architecture had spiraled into itself, exposing the tremendous effort of the Promethean architect as nothing but self-congratulatory irrelevance.

Aside from its institutional pertinence, Choi offered her own – very characteristic – explanation for her letter's success: "I think maybe architects liked the letter because it's so abusive and architects just like pain? Or they like any attention, even if it's bad?"

• • • • • • • •

However crass or sarcastic, Annie Choi's open letter made a pointed critique of the profession as a whole, unapologetically calling out the navel-gazing discourse and the irrelevance into which it has dissolved. In the letter she writes, "I have a friend who is a doctor. He gives me drugs. I enjoy them. I have a friend who is a lawyer. He helped me sue my landlord. My architect friends have given me nothing. No drugs, no medical advice."[9] Choi rattles off a laundry list of grievances, from cramped apartments to sprawling malls, amounting to a portrait of the daily interactions with buildings experienced by the vast majority of humanity. Architects do nothing to address these very real, immediate concerns, despite those concerns being situated squarely in the purview of the architect. Academically and professionally, architects are disconnected.

There is a sharp asymmetry at play: people know what they need and want, yet architecture spins into navel-gazing and drifts farther and farther from the possibility of substantive contribution to the communities it is meant to serve. In his 1975 book *Soft Architecture Machines*, Nicholas Negroponte wrote that there is "a general feeling that architecture, particularly housing, has been inadequate and unresponsive to the needs and desires of its users…the design of housing is in the wrong hands, that is, in the hands of an outside 'professional' rather than that of the resident."[10] No one is more familiar with the user's needs than the users themselves, yet they are excluded from the process. The same substantive criticism existed in pre-modern architecture – the object of a rant in *The Dictionary of Accepted Ideas* compiled/authored by Gustave Flaubert (1821–80) – published at the turn of the 20th century: "Architects, all idiots; they always forget to put in the stairs."[11]

The objective of user-focused design has long motivated architects. The goal of modernism and the *Gesamtkunstwerk* approach was to resolve all of the deficiencies, inefficiencies, and inadequacies of architecture in one swift stroke. Considering the totality of human inhabitation as the object of design, the Promethean architect sought to reform modern man, from spoon to city, from city to society. That gleaming white purity of intention has, over the past century, been at best revealed as a chimera, and at worst forcefully shattered by the realities of habitation and society. Yet the profession clings to its scraps of messianic idealism, at once aloof and impotent.

The blame, however, is hard to place. In what amounts to a universal tangle of finger-pointing, specific issues are shunted between participants in the design/construction/inhabitation process until human relevance is lost in the mix. Almost all governments, for example, promote the construction of more energy-efficient buildings, but effectively pass the baton to development organizations that (logically) see higher energy performance purely as a cost. The only person with a direct economic interest in designing for better energy performance is the person who will pay the energy bills[12]...and the only way that person can exercise control is to shut off the heater and shiver through winter. The general principle applies very tangibly to nearly every aspect of design.

An analogy is a child playing at the beach – completely absorbed in crafting the most magnificent sand-castle that the shoreline has ever known, he works with his back to the sea...

where, unbeknownst to him, a terrific wave looms, poised to crash. As the consummate American designer and theorist "Bucky" Fuller (1895–1983) ominously proclaimed in 1969, "Whether it is to be Utopia or Oblivion will be a touch-and-go relay race right up to the final moment.... Humanity is in a 'final exam' as to whether or not it qualifies for continuance in Universe."[13] It is, perhaps, dramatic to swell architectural practice to the scale of the universe as a whole, but the same urgency certainly projects onto the rising tensions in human habitation. Architecture is, by necessity, at the brink of another revolution.

With the lack of user participation echoing throughout the history of modern architecture – and as users drift ever farther from the design process today – new open-source models for a collaborative approach may have dramatic implications. From software to fab labs, open-sourcing has emerged as a powerful new mode for engagement. The pressing question is how to reorient architectural practice toward people, and the answer will be to put architecture into the hands of those people themselves. Has the moment for a new, relational and less hierarchical form of production finally arrived?[14]

This amounts to a galvanic call for action. Ethel Baraona-Pohl maintains that "the time has come to transform dissatisfaction into serious proposals, to start taking back the city for the citizens, to remove the distinction between public and private in the urban environment, to go from DIY (do it yourself) to DIWO (do it with others)."[15] No doubt an extreme position, but there may yet be a future for architecture designed by humanity, for humanity.

In the course of this revolution, as control returns to the crowd, must the architect be guillotined? Does this toll the death of his Promethean figure? He can only survive through adaptation – and if he is successful, what will be his role?

This central question – a redefinition of the architect – has been explored from many angles by architects and thinkers since the 1960s. In a prescient answer, Nicholas Negroponte predicted the evolution of the designer into a "middle man": a creator of open frameworks rather than deterministic forms. The process of architecture "would not be a case of reckless autocracy; rather, it would be a pervasive and evasive set of restrictions,"[16] suggesting a fundamental transformation of architectural deliverables. Rather than providing a finite and buildable design, the architect would determine a set of parameters that direct a flourishing body of ideas, a nearly infinite spectrum of potential architecture. Architects would design the question, not the response. Citing French architect and designer of the "*Ville spatiale*" (The Spatial City, 1958) Yona Friedman, Negroponte wrote, "The paternalistic character of the traditional design processes will disappear. The enormous variety of emotional (intuitive) solutions which can be invented by a large number of future users might give an incredible richness to this new 'redesigned' design process."[17]

Concerned with – in the words of Hans Ulrich Obrist – "flexibility, responsiveness, transience, relativity, joy,"[18] Cedric Price worked toward a similar reconfiguration of the architect's role, forging an idea of the architect as programmer. In projects such as *Potteries Thinkbelt* (1965), *The Generator* (1976), and the *Magnet Project* (1997), the architect provided a set of algorithms, provocations and interactions. "In Price's view, the architect should not be content with being a mere designer of hardware, but should demand an even broader responsibility for creating activity programs and determine how they could be integrated."[19] Obrist focuses on Price's key architectural contribution as the activation of space, rather than its creation. "The idea is not to occupy space, but to trigger relations and social spaces, stimulate new patterns and situations of urban movement in the city."[20] The architect offered event rather than form.

Beginning in the early 20th century, the emergent discipline of cybernetics sought to explore network systems, focusing on the communication and connections between interdependent nodes – and it offered the language in which Price would define the architect-as-programmer, in a fertile collaboration with pioneering cybernetician Gordon Pask. In *The Architectural Relevance of Cybernetics* (1969), Pask was one of the first to apply the conceptual framework of cybernetics to architecture, largely through discourse and collaboration with Price. "We are concerned with brain-like artifacts," wrote Pask, "with evolution, growth and development; with the process of thinking and getting to know about the world. Wearing the hat of applied science, we aim to create...the instruments of a new industrial revolution – control mechanisms that lay their own plans."[21] When exercised in architecture, cybernetics was less about designed, artistic, object-buildings than architectural scripts for adaptive ecologies that evolve through a form of dialogue with inhabitants.

Price was discarding architectural precedent, in favor of architecture as event. Conversely, N. John Habraken suggested that the redesigned design process would be discovered by the architect only through close scrutiny of the characteristics and tendencies embedded in the existing fabric of architecture – that is, considering the built environment as an autonomous entity (see earlier discussions in Chapter 2).[22] Throughout the history of architecture, as Habraken points out, building design has evolved on the timescale of generations. In the traditional evolution of vernacular architecture, a person may design her house to be similar to the neighbors', but with slight modifications and improvements. After a project is built, it is evaluated by the community, even unconsciously, and subsequent projects will modify and innovate. So architecture propagates and evolves, based on typologies, shared information and subtle experimentation – from Native American dwellings to Gothic cathedrals.

As Habraken articulated in *The Structure of the Ordinary* (1998),[23] willful architectural intervention should be predicated on diagnosis, just as a medical doctor studies the human body before he administers treatment. Based on a process of examining and analyzing the existing built environment, an architect can ultimately create frameworks that cultivate user-generated design, leading to "three-dimensional urban design." A project is not a grand act of creation in and of itself, but a single link in a much longer evolutionary chain. The role of the architect, in Habraken's estimation, is closer to that of a gardener. He learns horticulture, surveys the land, creates planter beds, and nurtures the plants that inhabit them. He is in partnership with inhabitants, rather than simply delivering a product. He leaves the most intimate material element of the built environment (house, work unit) to be the sole purview of users themselves. In this way, the living cells of architecture correspond directly to the individual in what Habraken calls a "natural relation." The architect has an opportunity to participate in the evolution of the autonomous built environment through creating frameworks within which users design.

This is not traditional on-paper participation at the level of urban planning, and users are not embroiled in the politics of the overarching project as a whole. The key point, as Alastair Parvin notes, is to make a "distinction between group, consensus-based collaboration (which is almost impossible) versus a more plural, permissive, shared-protocol-based approach, in which individuals are more or less autonomous, but operate within basic common rules, and copy from each other (which is almost inevitable)."[24] It is a delicate process of independent but interconnected production, with the architect serving as gardener, catalyzing the collective–individual scale. People can inhabit naturally, based on their preferences, yet exist harmoniously in the shared space of a single building. The architecture that people encounter, says Habraken, is "a living cell where the nominal social unit interacts without mediation with the smallest material unit recognizable as a changeable whole."[25] That is, people have agency in their own environment, which, collectively, constitutes the driver of the evolutionary process: "Ultimately, once the living cell is capable of individual action to adapt or renovate, both invention and sustainability can penetrate rapidly in the entire body of an environmental fabric. At that point the network among inventors and designers – including lay people – can fully develop its true potential."[26]

Habraken's model, first posited in the 1970s, was prescient of production models that are only just coming into their own. Many of the collaborative experiments that have emerged on the Internet, such as Linux or Wikipedia, utilize a very similar distributed generative mechanism, but with a key difference: the autonomy of the individual contributors is guided, moderated and nurtured by editors who can make decisions from the top down. This editorial role, more than that of a gardener, a middle-man or a programmer, has a broader orchestrating function. He will have qualities of each, but simultaneously take on an entirely new character, in the context of a digital and networked world. It is a plural figure that could be called "the Choral Architect."

As it outlines a new kind of designer, the idea of a Choral Architect brings with it a host of related questions. What tools and methods can direct dispersed energy in a way that transforms a crowd into a cohesive, motivated, and productive entity? How can a broad network of people, working together, arrive at a buildable and relevant architectural design? And if that is the goal, how is the Choral Architect different from the principal of a corporate architecture firm? In light of this plural creative model, what is the specific role of the Choral Architect?

The first and most fundamental responsibility of the Choral Architect is to frame the process. Just as Torvalds did with Linux, the Choral Architect must begin by generating a "kernel" that is subsequently distributed, iterated and added to. Without an impetus, the crowd will default to Brownian motion. By the same token, Giuliano da Empoli suggests that one of the most important tasks is actually to end the collaborative production. "A new and better idea might emerge from the network a day, or a week after the project is closed. But he has to do it, otherwise nothing will ever get built...this prerogative is an essential one. It should be included in his job description."[27]

Da Empoli implies that the Choral Architect is also responsible for steering the project by making often-difficult decisions and defining the rhythm of its development. He has a role as arbiter in the situations when consensus cannot be reached – again, much like the team of editors that guides Linux through a tumult of input. In some cases, the editorial hand needs to be incisive (more similar, perhaps, to that great critical tool that Ernest Hemingway described as his "built-in, shock-proof, bullshit detector").[28] He is also responsible for setting the pace of the entire process, deliberately orchestrating the moments of openness and collaboration versus closed honing and decision-making. Within these capacities, the Choral Architect might also integrate his own esthetic or functional ideas, contributing expertise and personality to the specific project.

The output of an architect, then, would not necessarily be buildings or construction documents, but initiating, coordinating, and closing the process whereby architectural source code is shared, adapted and executed. The Choral Architect will orchestrate actions and interactions naturally emerging from a group of peers – and therein is the difference with the principal of a corporate architecture firm – rather than creating objects. In framing the work of a co-design lab at Sitra, Alejandro Aravena wrote, "A good strategic framework will not precisely predict a single solution, but will help the best solution seem self-evident when identified."[29] Yet this does not at all mean an abdication of responsibility or even "signature" from a given project, any more than it does for an art curator. Arguably, the curator's voice is just as prominent as the artists', but in a more diplomatic role: steering the meaning of an exhibition through proximities, juxtapositions and pairings, rather than speaking through a brush and paint.

If architecture can operationalize a similar design–curation ecosystem, each instance of this networked editorial creative process would be unique. A project would derive from the peculiarities of the particular group and the context it is working in, draw on the tremendous power of the network, and be moderated by the Choral Architect. Because the content of a project is not singularly generated (as in the author model), and because evolution happens within its lifetime, the choral approach yields surprising results. Valuable – and previously voiceless – insights will be aggregated and instrumentalized in the process of design. As the power of the crowd comes to bear on specific problems, the global could in effect mediate with the local, addressing some of the problems inherent in so-called "Critical Regionalism" – specifically, the irrelevance of a starchitect copying and pasting his characteristic style indiscriminately across regions or the blandness of standardized, anesthetized architectural products. The collaborative online design process brings together voices to create a kind of "Network Specifism."[30]

Contemporary network technologies give rise to robust and productive curation ecologies, just as in open-source software. But ultimately that global collaborative energy must be funneled into bricks-and-mortar architecture. The role of the

Choral Architect is also to maintain and orchestrate that mate-
rialization process. As it has always been, the built environment
becomes once again an autonomous entity, nudged in one direction or another by the processes of human inhabitation.

We can assert that design becomes plural – yet Habraken's
most incisive question, posed in response to the initial manuscript of *Open Source Architecture*, has still not been answered.
What is different now than at any time in the past? After all
of the frustrated efforts of involving users in the design process
throughout the 20th century, what will make this substantively
different? "That the digital revolution can and will play a role
I do not doubt, but...how can a creative network of design and
production driven by the digital revolution connect to the reality
of built environment's life and development?"[31]

There are several factors that are poised to ignite new
possibilities in architecture. First, information – the "code"
or DNA of a building – can be shared instantaneously and
a-spatially. The intellectual project of such groups as CIAM
(Congrès internationale d'architecture moderne, founded by
Le Corbusier in 1928) was to share thoughts, ideas, theory (or
code) and collaboratively to write a charter – but in order to do
so they had to rent a ship and sail across the Mediterranean, to
meet face-to-face. Today, collaborative writing happens effortlessly, implicating millions of people every second, around the
world, through platforms like Wikipedia. Recipes or formulas
for spatial phenomena can be considered as the software of architecture, notes Keller Easterling.[32] Just as in Wikipedia, Linux,
and open-source software, code can be shared, augmented and
refined before it is compiled and executed. Choral design ignites
the autonomy of the building process within a single project.
The kernel of architecture exists as data, is honed by a distributed sequence of adding and editing, and finally culminates in a
physical structure – the execution of code in space.

This kind of sharing can happen effectively now that a building "exists" digitally before it is constructed – promoting a radical change toward openness and distribution in the design process. Traditional and vernacular collaborative processes worked through discrete leaps, as mutation and improvement happened from one execution of the code to the next – and today that is changing.

In the case of cuisine, for example, there exist basic structures. For example, take bouillon – each time a specific soup is cooked, the structure is expanded and made unique, it is shared and eaten; and subsequently modified for the next dinner. The result of each experiment is evaluated, and information about the most successful developments is encoded in recipes to be distributed and replicated. Mutation only happens from one dish to the next. Yet today (in architecture), the ability to assess a building before it is built allows collaboration at every stage. To continue with the cooking metaphor, it is as if an individual soup itself were created collaboratively – that is, by many cooks experimenting together in the kitchen, constantly tasting their work.

In this case, the design process would edge closer to the model of science writing, wherein a piece is created by a team of contributors, legitimized through peer review, and distributed for wider application within the field. Work is developed collaboratively (necessarily, given the acceleration of complexity), while the scrutiny of peer review ensures quality and provides a stamp of credibility. In the course of its development from idea to publishing, a single paper experiences a rhythm of opening up to peer review and revision by the authors. It is a self-regulating, participatory and incentivized system.

This is the mandate of the Choral Architect. To contradict the standard adage – architectural cuisine will benefit from many cooks in the kitchen, integrated by a talented chef. Situated between Le Corbusier's authoritative, era-defining voice and the Internet's dispersed collective banter, a designer enmeshed in networked communities will make harmonies. The architect will not be anonymous, but plural and compositional. Authorship will not be erased, but contextualized as it is woven into a relational fabric. The new architect is situated between top-down and bottom-up, channeling the raw energy of the latter through the targeted framework of the former. The responsibility of the Choral Architect is less oriented toward object-building than orchestrating process. She is not a soloist, not a conductor, not an anonymous voice among many. The Choral Architect weaves together the creative and harmonic ensemble.

• • • • • • • •

This chapter has traced the outline of a new Choral Architect – but, hypocritically, with the singular confidence of an assured diva. If we, the author(s), are sincere about these ideas, we won't be authors at all, but orchestrators of a vibrant dialogue. The text will grow in unexpected directions and at a faster pace if it takes the form of a wiki rather than remaining a monologue. Think of it not as a book, but as a debate, or a joke, or a brainstorming session.

With that, we turn it over to you....

7

. . . .

Over To You:
Go Ahead, Design!

If tomorrow's buildings and cities will now be more like computers – than machines – to live in, Open Source Architecture provides an open, collaborative framework for writing their operating software.

Various authors, "*Open Source Architecture*", 2011[1]

During the spring of 2011, *Domus* magazine was planning a special issue devoted to the concept of "open-source design." The issue would include articles on such topics as "The Esperanto of Objects," the architecture of Facebook, and a crowd-funded monument to RoboCop. When the editors asked Carlo Ratti to contribute an op-ed, he replied with a question: is it possible to write collaboratively? Especially given the subject – open sourcing – could the piece itself be open-sourced?

Eager to put authorship into many hands, he started a Wikipedia page on May 3, 2011, and sent invitations to an initial group of contributors, including Paola Antonelli, Hans Ulrich Obrist, Alex Haw, Nicholas Negroponte, N. John Habraken and Mark Shepard. His introductory email stated:

"I thought that the editorial itself should be written in an OPEN-SOURCE, collaborative way – and I thought that we could do it together! At the moment it is the seven of us (feel free to send suggestions about others who might join our effort!). Just to begin the process, I am enclosing some initial points below. Feel free to start adding/editing/...."[2]

Almost immediately, the page was opened up to the Internet at large, and thoughts, comments, and revisions began pouring in. What started as a few bullet points became an unstructured lump of text and then took shape under headings and sources and references. Yet nothing escapes the assiduous (and abundant) eyes of the Wikipedia community. As it grew, the Open Source Architecture page was red-flagged as an "opinion piece" by the editing collective and quickly deleted, on May 11, after only eight days of work.

Undeterred, the co-authors and adjunct editors polished and finalized the article offline until it was captured in print on May 18, 2011. The fight with Wikipedia editors ended when the piece was published in *Domus*, the paper copy adding legitimacy to its digital antecedents and progeny. What appears in the magazine is like a screenshot of a live-action film: a single instant, frozen for the sake of convenience, but pointing toward a far more interesting and dynamic whole. "Open Source Architecture," generated through a new writing process, skips between different media and over a range of scale, ultimately speaking with professional credibility, but without a singular byline.

Perhaps as a result of its distributed authorship, the process wasn't smooth, sharing wasn't seamless, and voices still shouted or whispered their own ideas. Comments circulated by email among the initial collaborators range from hilarious – "yo all, love the fact that the wikibods scheduled the article for deletion within minutes of its posting; the iterative question-marks of subsequent edits might accelerate its demise" or "the thing about the Korean sauce is not THAT funny..." – to legitimately critical of the process and broader concept of open sourcing – "I will add my bits and will be respectful of the rest but you might want to take the hatchet and the paintbrush in your hands at some point" and "Cooking is often hailed as an early form of open source." Some even simultaneously critical and playful, "i love the response to an open invite being a closed email; perfect!"

And then there was the issue of a headshot. Traditionally, *Domus* prints a photograph of each op-ed author with his article, so "Open Source Architecture" posed a problem. The editors initially approached Carlo Ratti, as it was he who had written the email to kickstart collaboration (and who had initially been commissioned), but in the end a simple profile shot did not seem right. Instead, *Domus* ran a digitally collated portrait of all the offline contributors – a race-and gender-ambiguous face, smiling as if it knows something we don't about the future of design.

Despite its tensions and mutations and ambiguities, the "Open Source Architecture" document remains live and open through Wikipedia and Creative Commons: the same active community of editors that had previously killed a nascent article now operates as a crowd of authors, continuing the conversation since it went to print. The Wikipedia page "Opensource [*sic*] Architecture" is in your hands. The text is fresh, relevant, and has a tingle of urgency – as the page continues to ferment it will grow and change in response to the new (hopefully networked and sociable) dimensions of architecture.

Despite its legitimization and accretion, the Wikipedia page today bears a standard (and somewhat comical) disclaimer in the heading:

"Warning

This article has multiple issues. Please help improve it or discuss these issues on the talk page.

This article possibly contains original research (June 2011)

This article's tone or style may not reflect the encyclopedic tone used on Wikipedia. (June 2011)"[3]

The publication of "Open Source Architecture" as an article (that is, the transition from Wikipedia to *Domus*) solicited a renewed tide of feedback, both from the editorial group and the public at large. Building on a swell of energy surrounding the theme of open-source architecture, we, the authors, were eager to push ideas further – to expand and explore the historical grounding and future possibility of open-source architecture – as a full book. And following the same logic that led to the original wiki, we decided to open the writing process to a plurality of authors.

Yet what manifested as minor hiccups and difficulties in the first writing processes, for the wiki and the *Domus* article, were correspondingly amplified and compounded in the longer-form book. What follows is the story of the text you read in this book.

Open Source Architecture the book began when the original authors – Carlo Ratti, Joseph Grima, and Tamar Shafrir, soon joined by Matthew Claudel – came together during the late spring of 2013 to expand the *Domus* article, enrich its ideas, and generate an outline for the full text. During subsequent months, this initial framework was bolstered with references and fleshed out into the first draft of a manuscript, in the hands of Ratti and Claudel. What was rough and conversational at first was iteratively sharpened through successive reviews and revisions.

With the manuscript to a coarse level of completion, the authors contacted a group of adjunct editors, soliciting feedback and augmentations to the text. Unlike the original Wikipedia page, this was a phased process of aggregating comments and incorporating them offline. Each editor was provided with an individual Google Doc keyed to line numbers in the manuscript, into which (s)he could insert specific content, to be digested and implemented by the authors in an organized way. Or, that is how it was envisioned.

In practice, feedback came in a wide variety of forms, from formally composed and addressed letters (N. John Habraken) to phone calls (Ricky Burdett) to sticky notes (Hans Ulrich Obrist). Heterogeneous and characteristic responses could be interpreted as either confusion or engagement...but invariably the editors freely interpreted the system (and some even rejected the system entirely, offering alternatives – as in Ethel Baraona-Pohl's emphatic support of "Bookie" as a co-working software).

Responses also came with varying levels of enthusiasm, from Giuliano da Empoli's final note, "I'm afraid you will probably find my comments a bit 'old style' and it is true that I am a little bit less enthusiastic about the wisdom of crowds than you seem to be," to Ethel Baraona-Pohl's line-by-line notes and accompanying message stating, "It reinforces the feeling of collective writing when some other person (even not knowing who) wrote the same thoughts you have, some times even better as you can do it. *Fantastique!*" Keller Easterling had an entirely different reaction to authorship – an impassable friction with the narrative voice that left her no choice but to formulate feedback as a disengaged letter addressing specific themes. As a preface, Easterling wrote, "I have been a bit uncertain about how to contribute. Wikis that add content into line edits often simply collect examples, amplifications or corrections. As I read the text, I did not find too many places where I had the urge to interrupt the voice.... When the voice is strong in the *Open Source Architecture* text, as it often is, it has the sense of a sustained argument with clear authorship. Thoughts that engage it in debate would have to stand aside, clarify their distance from the argument or risk unfairly putting words in the mouth of the authors. I would not want to do that.... Like Wikipedia or science writing, [my] arguments would perhaps be footnoted to distance them from the main voice and, more importantly, allow readers to access the additional information. Perhaps the whole thing constitutes a footnote? Or a gesture to a sister discourse? I really was not sure.... Wiki as encyclopedia is easier than wiki as manifesto."

The content of responses was far from cohesive as well – Alastair Parvin noted WikiHouse as a platform for the Choral Architect, while Alex Haw dismissed it as "not a house – it's a silly, useless, nonfunctional project with no surfaces & the most absurd junctions on the planet." In short, *Open Source Architecture* has become the ring in a wrestling match of ideas – sparring that could continue, seemingly indefinitely.

That question precisely – editing the flow of ideas and framing a work as complete – is a crucial role of the new "Choral Author," in the eyes of da Empoli. "In my mind," he wrote in a formal message, "the author has one critical responsibility, which is almost always overlooked: he is the one that decides when the book is finished. It's a huge responsibility." In lieu of a true wiki, the authors of this project have served as orchestrators of a complex (and convoluted) process, ultimately determining its final manifestation.

Another crucial role – particularly in the case of *Open Source Architecture* – was to find some way of crediting a motley assortment of contributions. In light of the varied responses (ultimately no two were the same) the authors decided on a crediting model that encompassed the variety of input, titled "adjunct editing." An initial (joke) email between authors on the subject of crediting read "maybe we don't even print HUO's name in the book? just a sticky on the inside cover of every copy – 'With adjunct editor Hans Ulrich Obrist' :-P."

The most difficult question of crediting, however, was within the author group itself. *Open Source Architecture* began as a collaboration between four, and the contract was signed accordingly: authorship was legally agreed as "Carlo Ratti and Joseph Grima, with Matthew Claudel and Tamar Shafrir." Yet over the eight-month writing process, Grima and Shafrir found themselves unable to contribute due to other obligations that arose. To honor the integrity of the open-source process, Grima suggested that the authorship be changed to "Carlo Ratti and Matthew Claudel," with Joseph Grima and Tamar Shafrir cited in the list of adjunct editors.

Traditional publishing structures are not, however, amenable to the vagaries of such an evolving open-source process. The very structure of the book project – based on a contract with an established publishing house that grants exclusive rights – is

almost antithetical to the ideas presented. The title page subverts
the book. The central idea of authorship catalyzed this inherent
tension: amidst all of the internal disjunction and miscommu-
nication, Andrea Bosco, the patient editor at Einaudi, watched
helplessly. The ramifications of altering a signed legal contract
were unpalatable, to say the least, and the discussion between
authors and editor sought a solution that was both honest and
equitable. Ultimately (after several months and dozens of email
flurries), the question was resolved with no ill feelings.

In retrospect – with edited, credited, and curated manuscript in hand – an unsettling question seems to follow the
thirteen names on the cover (many of whom have never met or
exchanged more than a few emails). How different would these
pages be without the Internet? How many years would it have
taken? What would have happened if we had all sat in the same
room? Could we have boarded a boat (or a cruise ship with well
stocked bar, à la CIAM) and disembarked holding the same text?

Similar projects in the past had a heavy overhead for
working together – simply coordinating logistics and travel for a
dozen contributors was a Titanic effort. For that reason, the ten
conferences of CIAM (and its ultimate dissolution at Congrès XI
in 1959) hold an unprecedented place of legend in architectural
history, as crowning moments of the modernist movement and
20th-century architecture as a whole. The epitome of CIAM
was the 1933 meeting held aboard a cruise from Marseilles to
Athens, during which the group, spearheaded by Le Corbusier,
produced the *Charte d'Athènes* (Athens Charter), published
a decade later, in 1943[4] – a radical and prescriptive urbanist
vision. Shortly thereafter, a fatal rift developed within CIAM,
from which a splinter group emerged – later to become known as
CIAM X, or "Team 10" – that proposed divergent ideas.

Team 10 had a subtly different approach. Although they
did meet in person a handful of times, the group was more

diffuse – a collection of architects and thinkers brought together by common ideas rather than international summits, more prone to releasing parallel but distinct individual pieces than mono-lithic manifestos. In its *Team 10 Primer*, editor Alison Smithson described the circle as "a small family group of architects who have sought each other out because each has found the help of the others necessary to the development and understanding of their own individual work."[5] The primer itself is a collection of essays, sent in by Team 10 members and curated by Smithson – in a way, a non-direct approach to outlining the team's ideas by triangulating between many different voices.

Echoes from Team 10 resonate with the Choral Architect. The group collaborated through an analogue process, but one that nonetheless points toward the kinds of co-creation that are now possible with the Internet. Connectivity today is fluid, imme-diate and a-spatial. The writing process of this book, *Open Source Architecture*, hinged on the Internet for both organization and content – the four original authors were based on three different continents, and the adjunct editors are even more widely spread. The Internet allows asynchronous, round-the-clock conversations between many people, as ideas are thrown into the Cloud, nur-tured, pared, or mutated. Collaboration today has been pushed to radical extremes – spatially extended and temporally collapsed – as discussed in "Learning from the Network" (Chapter 4).

Does that also cheapen it? Perhaps the symbolic weight of physically coming together, as did CIAM on the cruise ship, lent urgency and gravity (and spectacle?) to a project, somehow galvanizing the ideas of the group. Can the best possible ideas be generated and communicated in a quick email? More impor-tantly, what provides incentive to contribute in a substantive way? And, given active participation, how is that energy directed? Could it ever be charged with the reactive energy shared by a crowd in real time?

The process of both coordinating and writing *Open Source Architecture* made clear the need for orchestration. Although vibrant, the kaleidoscopic latitude of contributions is not productive without direction. A crowd defaults to Brownian motion. It is lazy, as Torvalds is keen to point out, but often without the cunning of the fox (and indeed, even Linux is oriented by a team of governing fathers, under Torvalds, the grandfather). This book, specifically, would be unrealized by the initiative of the crowd – but by the same token, it would not exist, in its present form, through the efforts of a single person.

The project of this book, then, amounts to an appeal for merging the two methodologies, and gives a name to the entity who will realize it. The Choral Architect is situated between top-down and bottom-up: at the nexus of raw, generative potential and singular vision. *Open Source Architecture* has uncovered a torrent of histories, ideas and opinions, unvoiced before the catalytic note to contributors, "just a quick email to send you the attached invitation – it would be great to have you onboard for this project!" and ultimately knit together by focused authorial effort. A project like this one must be steered through the generative process by someone (or a team) with the will to see it succeed. In the case of *Open Source Architecture*, the process was a rhythm of expansion and contraction – opening up to broader input, then narrowing to sharpen the ideas. Intentional phasing kept the book moving and gave it a productive methodology.

The book itself is an experiment, a case study, and an analogy for the reconfigured creative processes of the future Choral Architect. Words are not bricks, and developing a text is profoundly different from designing architecture, but we believe that the same creative models will echo through both. Given their basis in tools of a similar ilk (networked, responsive and dynamic), the plural voice of *Open Source Architecture* and the Choral Architect may, ultimately, be singing the same tune.

• • • • • • • •

The following is the text that appeared in the *Domus* magazine.

OSArc (Open Source Architecture)[6]

OSArc (Open Source Architecture) is an emerging paradigm describing new procedures for the design, construction and operation of buildings, infrastructure and spaces. Drawing from references as diverse as open-source culture, avant-garde architectural theory, science fiction, language theory, and others, it describes an inclusive approach to spatial design, a collaborative use of design software and the transparent operation throughout the course of a building and city's life cycle.

Cooking is often hailed as an early form of open source; vernacular architecture – producing recipes for everyday buildings – is another form of early lo-fi open-source culture, openly sharing and optimising technologies for building. A contemporary form of open-source vernacular is the Open Architecture Network launched by Architecture for Humanity, which replaces traditional copyright restrictions with Creative Commons licensing and allows open access to blueprints. Wider Open Source Architecture relies on a digital commons and the shared spaces of the World Wide Web to enable instantaneous collaboration beyond more established models of competition and profit. Traditional architectural tools like drawings and plans are supplemented and increasingly replaced by interactive software applications using relational data and parametric connectivity.

Open Source Architecture is not only involved with production; reception to a given project – critical, public, client, peer-related – can often form part of the project itself, creating a feedback loop that can ground – or unmoor – a project's intention and ultimately becomes part of it, with both positive and negative consequences. Open Source Architecture supersedes architectures of static geometrical form with the introduction of dynamic and participatory processes, networks, and systems. Its proponents see it as distinguished by code over mass, relationships over compositions, networks over structures, adaptation over stasis. Its purpose is to transform architecture from a top-down immutable delivery mechanism into a transparent, inclusive and bottom-up ecological system – even if it still includes top-down mechanisms.

Open Source Architecture relies upon amateurs as much as experienced professionals – the genius of the mass as much as that of the individual – eroding the binary distinction between author and audience. Like social software, it recognises the core role of multiple users at every stage of the process – whether as clients or communities, designers or occupants; at its best, it harnesses powerful network effects to scale systems effectively. It is typically democratic, enshrining principles of open access and participation, though political variations may range from stealth authoritarianism to communitarian consensualism.

Open Source Architecture revolutionises every step of the traditional building process, from brief-building to demolition, programming to adaptive reuse, including the following:

Funding
New economic models, exemplified by incremental microdonations and crowd-funding strategies like Sponsume and Kickstarter, offer new modes of project initiation and development, destabilising the traditionally feudal hierarchy

of client/architect/occupant. Financing of private projects increasingly moves to the public domain, offering mass rather than singular ownership, whereas funding of public projects can be derived from more flexible, responsive frameworks than simple levies or taxation. Open Source Architecture has particular appeal for builders outside the mainstream economy, such as squatters, refugees, and the military.

Engagement

Traditional developments deploy engagement programmes in which the community is consulted on incoming developments, with blunt tools such as focus groups, which often result in lack of representation and input, or at worst can result in NIMBYism. With crowd-funded models, forms of engagement are built into the process, enabling a kind of emergent urbanism in which use of space is optimized on terms set by its users. This reclamation of people's power can be seen as a soft, spatial version of Hacktivism. Open Source Architecture can suffer some of the organizational drawbacks of open-source software, such as project bifurcation or abandonment, clique behaviour and incompatibility with existing buildings.

Standards

Standards of collaboration are vital to Open Source Architecture's smooth operation and the facilitation of collaboration. The establishment of common, open, modular standards (such as the grid proposed by the OpenStructures project) addresses the problem of hardware compatibility and the interface between components, allowing collaborative efforts across networks in which everyone designs for everyone. Universal standards also encourage the growth of networks of non-monetary exchange (knowledge, parts, components, ideas) and remote collaboration.

Design

*Mass customization replaces standardization as algorithms
enable the generation of related but differentiated species
of design objects. Parametric design tools like Grasshopper,
Generative Components, Revit and Digital Project enable
new user groups to interact with, navigate and modify the
virtual designs, and to test and experience arrays of options
at unprecedented low cost – recognizing laypeople as
design-decision-making agents rather than just consumers.
Open-source codes and scripts enable design communities
to share and compare information and collectively optimize
production through modular components, accelerating
the historical accumulation of shared knowledge. BIM
(Building Information Modelling) and related collaboration
tools and practices enable cross-disciplinary co-location of
design information and integration of a range of platforms
and timescales. Rapid prototyping and other 3D printing
technologies enable instant production of physical artefacts,
both representational and functional, even on an architectural
scale, to an ever-wider audience.*

Construction

*The burgeoning Open-Source Hardware movement enables
sharing of and collaboration on the hardware involved in
designing kinetic or smart environments that tightly integrate
software, hardware and mechanisms. Sensor data brings
live inputs to inert material and enables spaces to become
protoorganic in operation; design becomes an ongoing,
evolutionary process, as opposed to the one-off, disjointed
fire-and-forget methodology of traditional architecture.
Operating systems emerge to manage the design, construction,
and occupancy phases, created as open platforms that foster
and nourish a rich ecosystem of "apps." Various practices*

jostle to become the Linux, Facebook or iTunes of architectural software, engaging in "platform plays" on different scales rather than delivery of plans and sections. Embedded sensing and computing increasingly mesh all materials within the larger "Internet of things," evolving ever closer toward Bruce Sterling's vision of a world of spimes. Materials communicate their position and state during fabrication and construction, aiding positioning, fixing and verification, and continue to communicate with distributed databases for the extent of their lifetime.

Occupancy

Open Source Architecture enables inhabitants to control and shape their personal environment – "to Inhabit is to Design", as N. John Habraken put it. Fully sentient networked spaces constantly communicate their various properties, states and attributes – often through decentralised and devolved systems. System feedback is supplied by a wide range of users and occupants, often either by miniature electronic devices or mobile phones – crowd-sourcing (like crowd-funding) large volumes of small data feeds to provide accurate and expansive real-time information. Personalization replaces standardisation as spaces "intelligently" recognize and respond to individual occupants. Representations of spaces become as vital after construction as they were before; real-time monitoring, feedback and ambient display become integral elements to the ongoing life of spaces and objects. Maintenance and operations become extended inseparable phases of the construction process; a building is never "complete" in Open Source Architecture's world of growth and change. If tomorrow's buildings and cities will now be more like computers – than machines – to live in, Open Source Architecture provides an open, collaborative framework for writing their operating software.

References

— Botson, R. and R. Rogers. *What's Mine is Yours: The Rise of Collaborative Consumption*. HarperCollins, New York, 2010.

— Fuller, M. and U. Haque. "Urban Versioning System 1.0." In *Situated Technologies Pamphlet Series*, No. 2. Architectural League of New York, New York 2008.

— Habraken, N. John. *Supports—An Alternative to Mass Housing.* The Architectural Press, London and Praeger, New York, 1972.

— Haque, U. Open-Source Architecture Experiment. 2003–05.

— Kaspori, D. "A Communism of Ideas: Towards an Architectural Open-Source Practice." *Archis* 3 (2003): 13–17.

— Kelly, K. *Out of Control: The Rise of Neo-Biological Civilization.* Perseus Books, New York, 1994.

— Leadbeater, C. *We-think: The Power of Mass Creativity.* Profile Books, London, 2008.

— Nettime mailing lists: mailing lists for networked cultures, politics, and tactics.

— Open Building Network / Working Commission W104, "Open Building Implementation" of the CIB, The International Council for Research and Innovation in Building and Construction (meets in a different country every year since its first meeting in Tokyo in 1994).

— Banham, R., P. Barker, P. Hall, C. Price. "Non Plan: An Experiment in Freedom." *New Society* 338 (1969) 435–43.

— Shepard, M. (ed.). *Sentient City: Ubiquitous Computing, Architecture, and the Future of Urban Space.* MIT Press, Boston, Mass., 2011.

— Sterling, B. "Beyond the Beyond." Blog on Wired Magazine website: http://www.wired.com/category/beyond_the_beyond/.

Notes

Chapter 1
The Promethean Architect: A Modern(ist) Hero

001 Rand, Ayn. "The Soul of an Individualist." In *For the New Intellectual: The Philosophy of Ayn Rand*. Random House, New York, 1961, p. 82.

002 Le Corbusier. *Vers une architecture*. (Toward an Architecture.) G. Cres, Paris, 1923, p. 86 [author's translation].

003 *Architecture or Revolution!* was the provisional title of *Vers une architecture* as outlined in a letter to William Ritter, April 7, 1922.

004 Boesiger, Willi. *Le Corbusier et Pierre Jeanneret Oeuvre Complète, Vol. 1, 1910–1929*. Editions Girsberger, Zurich, 1930, p. 104 [author's translation].

005 Ibid.

006 Nieuwenhuys, Constant. *New Babylon – a Nomadic City*. Exh. cat. Haags Gemeentemuseum, The Hague, 1974.

007 Wolfe, Tom. *From Bauhaus to Our House*. Farrar, Straus & Giroux, New York, 1981, p. 23.

008 Parvin, Alastair. Personal communication as Adjunct Editor. January 2014.

009 Ledoux, Claude-Nicolas. *L'Architecture considérée sous le rapport de l'art, des mœurs et de la legislation*. (Architecture Considered in Relation to Art, Morals and Legislation.) Paris, 1804.

010 Anonymous. "Etudes d'architecture en France." (Studies of Architecture in France.) *Magasin Pittoresque*. Paris, 1852.

011 Ledoux, *L'Architecture considérée*.

012 Fourier, Charles. *Théorie de l'unité universelle.* (Theory of Universal Unity.) Paris, 1822.

013 Fourier, Charles. *La Réforme Industrielle ou Le Phalanstère, Journal des intérêts generaux, de l'industrie et de la propriété.* (Industrial Reform or The Phalanstery, Journal of General Interests, Industry and Property.) Paris, June 1, 1832 to February 28, 1834.

014 Bentham visited Russia in 1787, later publishing his letters to a friend with postscripts. Bentham, Jeremy. *The Panopticon Writings.* London, 1791, p. 103.

015 Ibid., p. 1.

016 Ibid.

017 Wagner, Richard. "Das Kunstwerk der Zukunft." (The Artwork of the Future.) Leipzig, 1849.

018 Gropius, Walter. *Manifest und Programm des Staatlichen Bauhauses.* (Bauhaus Manifesto.) Weimar, 1919.

019 Wolfe, *From Bauhaus,* p. 43.

020 Rand, *The Fountainhead.*

021 Le Corbusier, *Vers une architecture,* p. 262.

022 Rand, *The Fountainhead,* p. 739.

023 Shapiro, Gideon Fink. "Review of *G: An Avant-Garde Journal of Art, Architecture, Design, and Film 1923–1926.* Detlef Mertins, Michael W. Jennings, eds." *Domus* web, March 25, 2011.

024 Easterling, Keller. Personal communication as Adjunct Editor. December 2013.

025 Sudjic, Deyan. *The Edifice Complex: The Architecture of Power.* Penguin, London, 2006.

026 Habraken, N. John. "Questions that Will Not Go Away: Some Remarks on Long-Term Trends in Architecture and their Impact on Architectural Education." Keynote speech at 6th EAAE/ENHSA meeting of Heads of European Schools of Architecture, June 2003, in Hania, Krete, Greece. In *open house international* 31: 2 (June 2006).

027 Colomina, Beatriz. "Towards a Global Architect." *Domus* 946 (April 2011).

028 Easterling, Keller. *The Action is the Form: Victor Hugo's TED Talk.* Strelka Press, Moscow, 2012, p. 21.

029 Parvin, Alastair. Personal communication as Adjunct Editor. January 2014.

030 Haw, Alex. Personal communication as Adjunct Editor. January 2014.

031 Vanstiphout, Wouter. Interviewed by Rory Hyde, "Historian of the Present: Wouter Vanstiphout." *Australian Design Review* (August 2011).

032 Ibid.

Chapter 2
Bottom-Up Architectures: The Timeless Way of Building

001 Le Corbusier. Quoted by Philippe Boudon, *Pessac de Le Corbusier*, Dunod, Paris, 1969, p. 2. English trans., *Lived-In Architecture: Le Corbusier's Pessac Revisited*. MIT Press, Cambridge, Mass., 1972.

002 Vasari, Giorgio. *Le Vite de' più eccellenti pittori, scultori, e architettori da Cimabue insino a' tempi nostri*. (The Lives of the Most Excellent Italian Painters, Sculptors and Architects, from Cimabue to Our Times.) Lorenzo Torrentino, Florence, 1550, p. 89.

003 Ibid., p. 71.

004 Ibid.

005 Parvin, Alastair. Personal communication as Adjunct Editor. January 2014.

006 Rudofsky, Bernard. *Architecture Without Architects: A Short Introduction to Non-Pedigreed Architecture*. Museum of Modern Art (distr. Doubleday Press), New York, 1964.

007 Ibid.

008 Ibid., p.58

009 Habraken, N. John. Personal communication as Adjunct Editor. December 2013.

010 Rudofsky. *Architecture Without Architects*, p. 9.

011 Ibid, p. 7.

012 Ibid, p. 6.

013 Mau, Bruce, and the Institute Without Boundaries. *Massive Change*. Phaidon, New York, 2005.

014 Parvin, Alastair. Personal communication as Adjunct Editor. January 2014.

015 Habraken, N. John. Personal communication as Adjunct Editor. December 2013

016 Haw, Alex. Personal communication as Adjunct Editor. January 2014.

017 Mumford, Lewis. *The City in History: Its Origins, Its Transformations, and Its Prospects*. Harcourt, Brace & World Inc., New York, 1961, p. 90.

018 Quarles, Philip. *The Decline of American Cities: Lewis Mumford's "The City in History*." Radio segment on WNYC, November 2012. http://www.wnyc.org/story/206665-lewis-mumford/

019 Romano, Marco. "Saper vedere la città: forme e immagini" (How to Look and See a Town: Shapes and Images), in *L'Estetica della città europea* (Aesthetics of the European City). Einaudi Editore, Turin, 1993.

020 Belluschi, Pietro. Quoted by Rudofsky. *Architecture Without Architects*, pp. 8–9.

021 Habraken, N. John. Personal communication as Adjunct Editor. December 2013.

022 Ibid.

023 Morris, William. *The Gothic Revival II,* in E.D. LeMire (ed.).
     The Unpublished Lectures of William Morris, Detroit 1969, p. 91.

024 James, John. *Chartres: The Masons who Built a Legend.* Routledge & Keegan
     Paul, London and Boston, Mass., 1982, p. 143.

025 James, John. *The Master Masons of Chartres.* West Grinstead Publications,
     Leura, NSW Australia, 1991.

026 Ruskin, John. *The Seven Lamps of Architecture.* Smith, Elder, and Co.,
     London, 1849, p. 204. Project Gutenburg, 2011, p. 119.

027 Ibid.

028 Ibid.

029 Parvin, Alastair. Personal communication as Adjunct Editor. January 2014.

030 Peter Smithson. *Patio and Pavilion Re-Built: A Gothic Afterthought,* in
     "Places," VII, 1991, p. 3.

031 Price, Cedric, Reyner Banham, Paul Barker, and Peter Hall. "Non Plan:
     an Experiment in Freedom." *New Society* 338 (March 1969): 435–43.

032 Colomina, Beatriz. "Towards a Global Architect." *Domus* 946 (April 2011).
     http://www.domusweb.it/en/architecture/2011/04/30/towards-a-global-
     architect.html

033 Utida, Yositika. "Experimental Apartment Building in Osaka," *Domus* 819
     (October 1999), pp. 18–26.

034 Habraken, N. John. Personal communication as Adjunct Editor.
     December 2013.

035 Obrist, Hans Ulrich. Personal communication as Adjunct Editor.
     March 2014.

036 Price, Cedric. *Cedric Price: Works II.* Architectural Association, London,
     1984. Republished as *Cedric Price: The Square Book,* Wiley-Academy,
     London, 2003, p. 92.

037 Cedric Price Memorandum (1964). Document cited by Stanley Matthews,
     From Agit-Prop to Free Space: The Architecture of Cedric Price. Black Dog Press,
     London, 2007, p. 73.

038 Obrist, Hans Ulrich. Personal communication as Adjunct Editor.
     March 2014.

039 Baraona-Pohl, Ethel. Personal communication as Adjunct Editor.
     December 2013.

040 Zenetos, Takis. Quoted in Dimitris Papalexopoulos and Eleni Kalafati,
     Takis Zenetos: Visioni Digitali, Architetture Costruite. Edilistampa, Rome, 2006

041 de Carlo, Giancarlo. In Alison Smithson, *Team 10 Primer.* Studio Vista,
     London, 1968.

042 Ibid.

043 De Carlo, Giancarlo. *Architecture's Public*. Originally Published in *Parametro Magazine* 5 (1970). Trans. Benedict Zucchi, *Giancarlo de Carlo*. Butterworth, Oxford, 1992.

044 Maki, Fumihiko. "Investigations in Collective Form." Washington University St Louis, School of Architecture, Mo. Special Publication No. 2, June 1964, p. v.

045 Maki. "Investigations."

046 Ibid.

047 Alexander, Christopher. *The Timeless Way of Building*. Oxford University Press, Oxford, 1979, p. 7.

048 Ibid.

049 Haw, Alex. Personal communication as Adjunct Editor. January 2014.

050 Le Corbusier. Cited in Boudon, *Lived-in Architecture*.

051 Boudon, *Lived-in Architecture*.

052 Huxtable, Ada Louise, "Le Corbusier's Housing Project — Flexible Enough to Endure." *The New York Times*. March 15, 1981.

053 Ibid.

Chapter3
Why It Did Not Work: A Horse Designed by Committee

001 Alexander, Christopher. *The Oregon Experiment*. Oxford University Press, Oxford, 1975, p. 45.

002 Moore, Clement Clarke. Quoted in "Historic Documents on View; When Chelsea was Farmland," *The New York Times*. October 9, 1994.

003 Ibid.

004 Ibid.

005 Alexander. *The Oregon Experiment*.

006 Ibid.

007 Ibid.

008 A common adage, this is generally attributed to a *Vogue* article. Issigonis, Alec. *Vogue* (July 1958).

009 Bryant, Greg. "The Oregon Experiment after Twenty Years." *Rain Magazine* 14:1 (Winter/Spring 1991).

010 De Carlo, Giancarlo. *Architecture's Public*. Originally published in *Parametro Magazine*, no. 5 (1970). Translated by Benedict Zucchi, *Giancarlo de Carlo*. Butterworth, Oxford, 1992.

011 Bryant, "The Oregon Experiment."

012 Alexander, Christopher. *The Nature of Order: An Essay on the Art of Building and the Nature of the Universe. Book Three: A Vision of a Living World.* The Center for Environmental Structure, Berkeley, Calif., 1980. The first two volumes were more about the pattern language, and the third was a critical look at its implementation.

013 Alexander, *The Nature Book Three,* p. 261.

014 Ibid.

015 Simon, Herbert A. *The Sciences of the Artificial.* MIT Press, Cambridge, Mass., 1969.

016 Archer, L. Bruce. *Systematic Method for Designers.* The Council of Industrial Design, London, 1965.

017 "The Design Method" in Birmingham (1965) and "Design Methods in Architecture" in Portsmouth (1967), both UK.

018 Rittel, Horst. Quoted by Churchman, C. West, "Guest Editorial." *Management Science* 14:4 (December 1967): 141–42.

019 Rittel, Horst and Melvin Webber. "Dilemmas in a General Theory of Planning." *Policy Sciences* 4 (1973) 155–69.

020 Ibid.

021 Blundell-Jones, Peter with Jeremy Till and Doina Petrescu. *Architecture and Participation.* Spon Press, Oxford and New York, 2005.

022 Sanoff, Henry. *Community Participation Methods in Design and Planning.* Wiley, New York, 1999.

023 Bryant, "The Oregon Experiment."

024 Habraken, N. John. Personal communication as Adjunct Editor. December 2013.

025 Ibid.

026 Habraken, N. John. *Supports: an Alternative to Mass Housing.* The Architectural Press, London, and Praeger, New York, 1972. (Originally published in Dutch under the title: *De Dragers en de Mensen.* Scheltema en Holkema, Amsterdam, 1962.)

027 Maki, Fumihiko. *Investigations in Collective Form.* Washington University St Louis, School of Architecture, Mo. Special Publication No. 2, June 1964.

028 Ibid., p. 11.

029 Castroni, Marco. "Refurbishing the '60s Masterpieces: La Rinascente and Corviale, Rome," *Arch Daily.* February 21, 2009.

030 Smithson, Alison and Peter. *Streets in the Sky.* Project on Robin Hood Gardens presented at CIAM IX Conference, Aix-en-Provence, France, July 1953.

031 Green, Steve. Comment on the article "Robin Hood Gardens Compulsory Purchase Plans Approved." *BD Online.* August 2012.

032 Alison, Charles and Obadiah Chambers. Quoted in "Row Over
     'Street in Sky' Estate." *BBC News* website. March 7, 2008.

033 Smithson, Peter. Interviewed by Maxwell Hutchinson, "Rebuilding
     Britain for the Baby Boomers." BBC Radio 4. November 26, 2011.

034 Tange, Kenzo. NHK Programme. January 1961.

Chapter 4
Learning From the Network:
New Paradigms for Participation in the Digital World

001 McLuhan, Marshall and Quentin Fiore (illus.). *The Medium is
     the Massage.* Bantam, New York and London, 1967, p. 12.

002 Torvalds, Linus. Bulletin Board news:comp.os.minix, August 26, 1991.

003 Torvalds, Linus. "Torvalds on git." Lecture at Google Tech Talk.
     May 2007.

004 Haw, Alex. Personal communication as Adjunct Editor. January 2014.

005 Sennett, Richard. *The Craftsman.* Allen Lane/Penguin, London; Yale
     University Press, New Haven; Berlin Verlag, Berlin; Feltrinelli, Milan,
     2008; Albin Michel, Paris and Anagrama, Barcelona, 2009.

006 Torvalds, Linus. "linux-kernel" posting (http://marc.info/?l=linux-
     kernel&m=137392506516022&w=2). July 15, 2013.

007 Torvalds, Linus. "The Way We Live Now: Questions for Linus Torvalds."
     The New York Times. September 28, 2003.

008 These were: The Declaration of Independence (1776), The Treaty of
     Alliance (1778), The Treaty of Paris (1782), and The United States
     Constitution (1787).

009 Franklin, Benjamin. *The Private Life of the Late Benjamin Franklin...Originally
     Written by Himself, and Now Translated from the French.* J. Parsons, London,
     1793. (First published as *Mémoires de la vie Privée de Benjamin Franklin,
     Écrits par Lui-Méme, et Adressés a Son Fils.* Chez Buisson, Paris, 1791.)
     In J. Bigelow (ed.), *The Works of Benjamin Franklin,* Knickerbocker,
     New York, 1904, p. 237.

010 Ibid., p. 238.

011 McLuhan, Marshall. *The Gutenberg Galaxy: The Making of Typographic Man.*
     University of Toronto Press, Toronto and Buffalo, New York, 1962.

012 Stearn, Gerald Emmanuel (ed. and comp.). *McLuhan Hot & Cool: a Primer
     for the Understanding of & A Critical Symposium with a Rebuttal by McLuhan.*
     Dial Press, New York, 1967, pp. 314–15.

013 Berners-Lee, Tim (27 July 2012). "This is for everyone." Twitter.
     Retrieved October 18, 2014.

014 McLuhan, Marshall. Letter to Harold Adam Innis, March 14, 1951.
     In Eric McLuhan and Frank Zingrone (eds.), *Essential McLuhan.*
     Anansi, Concord, Ontario, 1995, p. 73.

015   Kelty, Christopher. *Two Bits: The Cultural Significance of Free Software.*
      Duke University Press, Durham, N. Car., 2008, p. 6.

016   Parvin, Alastair. Personal communication as Adjunct Editor. January 2014.

017   Barksdale, Jim. "Netscape Announces Plans to Make Next Generation
      Communicator Source Code Available Free on the Net," Netscape
      Communications Corporation Press Release. January 22, 1998.

018   Kelty, *Two Bits*, p. 12.

019   McCarthy, Tom. "Encyclopedia Britannica Halts Print Production
      After 244 Years," *The Guardian*. March 13, 2012.

020   Chesky, Brian. Interviewed by Thomas Friedman, "Welcome to the
      Sharing Economy." *The New York Times*. July 20, 2013.

021   Bacon, Derek. "The Rise of the Sharing Economy." *The Economist*.
      March 9, 2013.

022   http://googlesystem.blogspot.sg/2013/06/google-mine.html

023   Veblen, Thorstein. *The Theory of the Leisure Class.* Macmillan, 1899.

024   Barr, Stewart. "Strategies for Sustainability: Citizens and Responsible
      Environmental Behaviour." *Area* 35:3 (September 2003): 227–40.

025   Sandel, Michael. *What Money Can't Buy: the Moral Limits of Markets.*
      Farrar, Straus and Giroux, New York, 2012.

026   Parvin, Alastair. Personal communication as Adjunct Editor. January 2014.

027   Huang, Carol. "Facebook and Twitter Key to Arab Spring Uprisings."
      The National (UAE). June 6, 2011.

028   Ibid.

029   "England Riots: Twitter and Facebook Users Plan Clean-up."
      The Guardian, August 9, 2011.

030   riotcleanup.co.uk.

031   Erdo du, Aysu. Quoted in Emrah Güler, "Sharing and Gift Economies
      Bloom in Turkey." *Hurriyet Daily News*. July 22, 2013.

Chapter 5
Open Source Gets Physical:
How Digital Collaboration Technologies Became Tangible

001   Gershenfeld, Neil. "Unleash Your Creativity in a Fab Lab."
      TED Lecture. February 2006.

002   Gershenfeld, Neil. Grassroots Invention Group. http://gig.media.mit.edu/

003   Gershenfeld, Neil. "Unleash Your Creativity."

004   Ibid.

005   Ibid.

006   Ibid.

007   Parvin, Alastair. Personal communication as Adjunct Editor. January 2014.

008   Kelty, Christopher. *Two Bits: The Cultural Significane of Free Software*.
      Duke University Press, Durham, N. Car., 2008, p. 29.

009   Parvin, Alastair. Personal communication as Adjunct Editor. January 2014.

010   Irvine, James. *Enzo Mari, Product + Furniture Designer. Celebrating 25 Years
      of Design*. Exh. print material, Design Museum London, March 29–June 22,
      2007.

011   Chin, Andrea. "Enzo Mari Autoprogettazione for Artek." *Design Boom*.
      April 8, 2010. http://www.designboom.com/design/enzo-
      mariautoprogettazione-for-artek/

012   Stallman, Richard. "GNU Manifesto." *Dr. Dobb's Journal* 10:3 (March 1985).

013   Casserly, Cathy. *The Future of Creative Commons*. Press statement.
      June 2013.

014   Shirky, Clay. "Re: (decentralization) Generalizing Peer Production
      into the Physical World." Yahoo! Groups forum post. November 5, 2007.
      https://groups.yahoo.com/neo/groups/decentralization/conversations/
      topics/6967.

015   The OS Car Project website. http://www.theoscarproject.org/

016   Open Source Green Vehicle website. http://p2pfoundation.net/Open_
      Source_Green_Vehicle

017   Free Beer website. http://freebeer.org/blog/

018   Arthur, Charles. "Technophile." *The Guardian*. February 27, 2008.
      See also Neuros website. http://www.neurostechnology.com/

019   RepRap website. http://reprap.org.

020   "Re: Looking for Your Thoughts." Rep Rap forum. June 2008.
      Forumsreprap.org.

021   Antonelli, Paola. "States of Design 03: Thinkering," *Domus* 948
      (June 2011).

022   Ibid.

023   Ibid.

024   Price, Cedric. "Life Conditioning," *Architectural Design* 36 (October 1966)
      483–94.

025   Sinclair, Cameron. "My Wish: A Call for Open-Source Architecture."
      TED Lecture. February 2006.

026   Open Architecture Network website. http://openarchitecturenetwork.org/

027   Sinclair, Cameron. "My Wish: A Call for Open-Source Architecture."
      TED Lecture. February 2006.

028   WikiHouse website. www.wikihouse.cc.

029   Parvin, Alastair. Personal communication as Adjunct Editor. January 2014.

030   Lerodiaconou, Nick. Quoted by Suzanne Labarre in "WikiHouse, An Online
      Building Kit, Shows How to Make a House in 24 Hours." *FastCo Design*
      (August 2011).

031   Kickstarter website. http://www.kickstarter.com/

032   Sitra website. http://www.sitra.fi/en

033   Hill, Dan and Bryan Boyer, *Brickstarter,* Sitra, 2013.
      http://brickstarter.org/Brickstarter.pdf

034   Goteo website. goteo.org/

035   Baraona-Pohl, Ethel. Personal communication as Adjunct Editor.
      December 2013.

036   Estate Guru website. http://www.estateguru.eu/

037   Parvin, Alastair. Personal communication as Adjunct Editor. January 2014.

038   Boissière, Olivier. "Editorial: Being Jean Nouvel." *Abitare* 518
      (December 2011).

039   Pavlus, John. "The Eames Studio's Inspiring History and Unknown
      Dark Side." *FastCo Design*. November 9, 2011.

040   Mirviss, Laura. "Starchitects Face Off in New Film." *Architectural Record*.
      April 2013.

041   Zara, Janelle. "Jean Nouvel, Frank Gehry and More Star in the
      Documentary Where Architects Stop Being Polite and Start Being Real."
      Blouin Art Info. April 2013.

042   WikiHouse website. Wikihouse.cc.

043   Markillie, Paul. "A Third Industrial Revolution." *The Economist*.
      April 21, 2012.

044   Parvin, Alastair. Personal communication as Adjunct Editor. January 2014.

Chapter 6
Building Harmonies: Toward a Choral Architect

001   De Carlo, Giancarlo. *Architecture's Public*. Originally published in *Parametro
      Magazine*, No. 5, 1970. Translated by Benedict Zucchi, *Giancarlo de Carlo*.
      Butterworth, Oxford, 1992.

002   Choi, Annie. Personal correspondence with Matthew Claudel. August 27,
      2013

003   Choi, Annie. "Dear Architects." *Pidgin Magazine* 2 (2007).

004   Choi, Annie. *Happy Birthday or Whatever: Track Suits, Kim Chee, and Other
      Family Disasters*. Harper, New York, 2007.

005   Choi, correspondence with Claudel.

006   Ibid.

007   Ibid.

008   Choi, "Dear Architects."

009   Ibid.

010   Negroponte, Nicholas. *Soft Architecture Machines*. MIT Press, Cambridge, Mass., 1975.

011   Flaubert, Gustave. Trans. Jacques Barzun. *The Dictionary of Accepted Ideas*. New Directions, New York., 1968. (First published as *Dictionnaire des idées reçues*, in French. Paris, 1911.)

012   Parvin, Alastair. Personal communication as Adjunct Editor. January 2014.

013   Buckminster Fuller, Richard. *Utopia or Oblivion*. Bantam Books, New York, 1969.

014   Baraona-Pohl, Ethel. Personal communication as Adjunct Editor. December 2013.

015   Ibid.

016   Negroponte, *Soft Architecture Machines*, p. 102.

017   Friedman, Yona. Cited in Negroponte, *Soft Architecture Machines*, p. 103.

018   Obrist, Hans Ulrich. Personal communication as Adjunct Editor. March 2014.

019   Ibid.

020   Ibid.

021   Pask, Gordon. "The Architectural Relevance of Cybernetics," *Architectural Design* (September 1969): 494–96.

022   Habraken, N. John. Personal communication as Adjunct Editor. December 2013.

023   Habraken, N. John. *The Structure of the Ordinary: Form and Control in the Built Environment*. MIT Press, Cambridge, Mass., and London, 1998.

024   Parvin, Alastair. Personal communication as Adjunct Editor. January 2014.

025   Habraken, N. John. Personal communication as Adjunct Editor. December 2013.

026   Ibid.

027   Da Empoli, Giuliano. Personal communication as Adjunct Editor. January 2014.

028   Hemingway, Ernest. Interview by George Plimpton, "The Art of Fiction, No. 21." *The Paris Review* 18 (Spring 1958): 76–77.

029   Aravena, Alejandro. Cited in Justin Cook and Bryan Boyer, *Designing Social Housing but Building Wealth. Case Study: From Shelter to Equity*. Helsinki Design Lab–Sitra, Helsinki 2012.

030   Ratti, Carlo; Claudel, Matthew; Haw, Alex; Picon, Antoine. "The Power
      of Networks: Beyond Critical Regionalism." *Architectural Review*, July 2013.
      http://www.architectural-review.com/view/the-power-of-networks-beyond-
      critical-regionalism/8651014.article

031   Habraken, N. John. Personal communication as Adjunct Editor.
      December 2013.

032   Easterling, Keller. Personal communication as Adjunct Editor.
      December 2013.

Chapter 7
Over To You: Go Ahead, Design!

001   Various Authors. "Open Source Architecture (Open Source Architecture)."
      Domus 948 (June 2011).

002   Ratti, Carlo. Email to Paola Antonelli, N. John Habraken, Alex Haw,
      Nicholas Negroponte, Hans Ulrich Obrist, and Mark Shepard. May 3, 2011.

003   Wikipedia website: http://en.wikipedia.org/wiki/Opensource_Architecture.

004   Le Corbusier. *La Charte d'Athènes* (Athens Charter). Éditions de
      l'architecture d'aujourd'hui, Collection de l'équipement de
      la civilisation machiniste, Boulogne-sur-Seine, 1943.

005   Smithson, Alison (ed.). *Team 10 Primer*. Studio Vista, London, 1968.

006   Various, "Open Source Architecture (Open Source Architecture)."

Index